Sustainable Growth Through Sustainable Business

Christopher Gleadle

ISBN: 1460929993
ISBN-13:9781460929995

DEDICATION

Ann

CONTENTS

Acknowledgments   i

1   What it's all about   5

Introduction

Climate change

Cost saving and the business contribution

What are your emissions?

Setting a strategy

Developing a sustainability plan

Conduct a baseline assessment

Creating a policy

Developing a policy

Implementation of the action plan

Sustainable procurement

Relationship and customer expectation compliance

2   Green Buildings and Smart Buildings   43

Introduction

Lighting

Energy monitoring and reduction

IT and data centers

Planning

Hot isles and cold isles

CACS

HACS

Therefore

Water management

Measurement verification and reporting

How to reduce water use

Landscaping

3	Communication	72
4	Offsetting	76
5	Investor risk and opportunity	78
6	Conclusions	88
7	Appendices 1 – 8	92

1) Infrastructure- where we are going and what it means to you

2) Offsetting projects and standards - Rainforests, Biomass, Methane recovery, Heat recovery, Water treatment, Wind farms, Hydro, Landfill gas recovery, Geothermal, Solar, Project conclusions

3) Development of new markets

4) Global warming potential

5) Deforestation of Borneo 1900 – 2005

6) Save our home

7) Websites of further interest

8) Glossary of terms

8	About the author	147

ACKNOWLEDGMENTS

For all family and friends who have supported me on this journey.

1 WHAT IT'S ALL ABOUT

Introduction

Over the last ten years, with the steady increase in regulation, sustainability has become a new economics for businesses to remain vital. This is as true for SMEs as it is large corporates.

Silos in organisations act as barriers to achieving the return on eco-efficient investments. With the removal of the silos – and so the barriers - eco-efficiency is poised to become the biggest economic game-changer for organisations over the next twenty years.

Eco-efficiency is broadly defined as the delivery of competitively priced goods and services meeting the needs of society whilst progressively reducing the environmental impact and resource intensity of goods and services throughout their life cycle.

The drivers are the need to be seen, act and prove to be more environmentally and socially responsible to attract continued investment, drive innovation, lower costs; whilst, under-pinning brand and reputation. SMEs in the supply chain have felt they are immune from the legislation, therefore have lacked enthusiasm to invest in sustainability-focused processes. Yet, the market has shifted its attention to the supply chains because research has shown, as much as seventy percent of all business emissions come from the SME sector collectively. Experience has further shown, there are also great cost reductions and other sustainability opportunities contained in sustainable procurement policies. The Carbon Trust estimates that the UKs four million SMEs could collectively save £1.37bn a year.

SMEs that have embraced sustainability as part of core business practice, have typically flourished against peers as clear differentiation has been delivered.

The supportive benefits of sustainability have shown to deliver improved value through cost reduction and making other positive contributions to the triple bottom line of: economic, environmental and social; while, also having a profound effect on the top line from innovation and enhanced brand and reputation.

Sustainability is about delivering the balance between profit and the environment; yet, for sustainability to be truly effective, it must be delivered as a three dimensional process linked to corporate strategy. This link gives visibility, as sustainability becomes part of the overall planning, budgeting and accountability process.

Environmental footprinting and the importance of data capture are equal to how that data is used, measured and verified. For example: the process demonstrates the interdependence of functional areas within an organisation: what optimisation may have taken place in one area could well have created a negative impact on another.

What you don't measure – you can't manage. Therefore, what you measure badly - you will manage badly.

Success can be achieved and measured by developing sustainability into the culture and DNA of a business. Success needs to be qualified and quantified. To achieve this measure of accountability, a company must understand the value of the energy and environmental process across the organisation and its value chain. This understanding supports a process of continual improvement and the achievement of robust and meaningful reductions. Reduction in energy consumption, reduction in waste, reduction in environmental impact and water use: creating a more environmentally and socially aware, proactively positive organisation.

Understanding the organisation from an energy and waste perspective allows all the processes to be viewed horizontally, and by breaking down all the natural barriers and silos, greater understanding is accomplished for the interdependence of the functional areas that make up the whole. Therefore, sustainability is a holistic process.

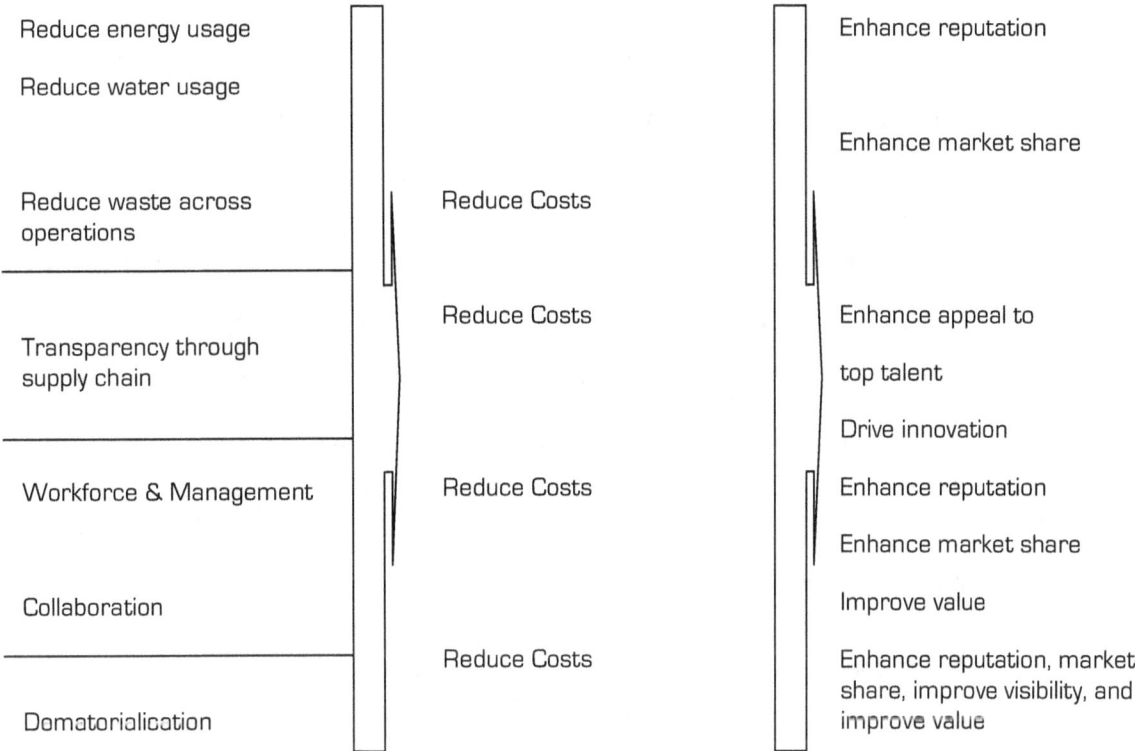

Create a sustainability baseline and embed into the overall corporate strategy because, a sustainability policy should be delivered as a three-dimensional process. This link gives visibility, as it becomes part of the overall planning, budgeting and accountability process. It becomes part of the corporate DNA delivering the balance between profit and the environment through eco-efficiency, creating innovation, helping drive sales and, strengthening brand and reputation.

Sustainability is more than just carbon footprinting. It brings the whole personnel structure together, from the boardroom to the storeroom. Sustainability is a quality stakeholder engagement process beginning inside the company where each person is responsible for a new metric defined around efficiency and the reduction of waste. Behavioral changes do not happen overnight; therefore, sustainability is a process in itself. Waste equals money.

It follows, in order to drive efficiency in the operations and infrastructure, efficiency in products and services through innovation will be achieved; improving the whole life cost of those products and services to the customer.

Additionally, for sustainability to be truly successful, the supply chain is a key element. It is important to understand the impact procured products and services have in terms of environmental impact to the organisation and to its customers. This gives great insight as to improvement in design and delivery; so, developing further, the benefits of reduced cost, stronger customer bonding and greater differentiation.

Sustainability and the addressing of the triple bottom line: economic, environmental and social is the only way forward, because it is a solid business case for growth.

A company's customers are going to be the main driver; however, there is legislation, typically addressing the largest polluters. That legislation is going to transcend the entire value chain, and it would be naive to think it will not. It would also be equally naive to think current legislation has nothing to do with organisations, which currently are not regulated. For current un-regulated businesses, they are in the value chain of those who are – the customers. Furthermore, the legislation horizon is constantly shifting towards tighter regulation for all, for example: in the UK, the Climate Change Act 2008. Legislation is global, and not limited to individual countries.

The supply chain is an area where reductions can be made. The supply chain is an area of risk-economically, environmentally and socially. Sustainable procurement practices, affect all.

Sustainability must to an extent sidestep science, politics and personal beliefs that can cloud the issues. Those who understand sustainability and embrace it - have and will - continue to deepen their engagement and advocacy with stakeholders, employees and customers.

It makes good business sense – but then, doing the right thing always has.

Climate Change

Climate Change is in the media constantly. Speak with friends, or colleagues, about Climate Change and everyone feels their knowledge is good. Yet, there is still a strong undercurrent of scepticism and how much is this going to cost me?

The business case for sustainability is proven, and the outside issues of science, politics and personal beliefs must be sidestepped, as they only cloud the issue. The only cost is not to embrace it into core business practice. So, whilst sustainability is not reliant on climate change belief one way or the other, it is important to understand something of the argument.

Climate Change is being brought about by the constant rise in Greenhouse Gases. These gases are produced by human activity and by the natural activity of the planet and all creatures on it.

The Earth is a living breathing entity in its own right, and for hundreds of millions of years, it has quite happily looked after itself, producing what we call Greenhouse Gases such as: Carbon Dioxide, Methane, Nitrous Oxide, Sulphurous Oxides. And, many others with which, I will not bore you.

Indeed, while the earth has created this background emission structure, it has been absorbing CO_2 through vast areas of forestation such as the tropical rainforests. We have always been educated that the tropical rainforests are the 'lungs of the world', absorbing CO_2 and breathing out Oxygen.

Furthermore, with a relative balance of climatic conditions, the earth has also reflected a great deal of solar radiation via the ice caps and frozen tundra of the extreme latitudes as the ice acts as large mirrors helping to keep temperatures in balance.

To help keep a balance, land and sea has also absorbed CO_2, and through geological time and the movement of landmasses, areas of frozen tundra and the vast ice sheets today retain inside them thousands of millions of tonnes of CO2. Scientists through using samples such as ice cores have measured this. By penetrating the ice sheets and taking the ice core samples, they have been able to measure CO2 concentrations trapped inside the ice going back hundreds of thousands of years.

Through the ability to take these samples, scientists can accurately measure CO2 concentrations accurately and hence terms such as ' Pre Industrial' and 'Post Industrial' concentrations can be stated with much certainty; mapping the human impact on the CO2 concentrations against the natural background emissions.

For ease, Greenhouse Gases are expressed always in terms of CO2 merely to give a constant to measure global warming by. For example: methane is twenty one times more powerful as a GHG than CO2 and has a Global Warming Potential twenty one times that of CO2; meaning that 1 tonne of Methane Emissions is equal to 21 tonnes of CO2 (21tCO2e).

Concentration, expressed as parts per million, is the measure of CO2 in the atmosphere and it is this concentration which restricts the radiant heat to escape out to space.

Pre Industrial levels measured by scientists using methods as previously discussed show a relatively regular concentration at 350ppm. Now this concentration is rising over 400ppm.

If concentrations are stabilised at 450ppm we could be looking at a temperature rise of about 2 degrees. By doing nothing, this figure could rise to 1000ppm by 2050 so driving a temperature rise of 5 to 10 degrees and untold catastrophic consequences. We must keep insight, such a stabilisation of 450ppm is on the back drop of rising industrialisation, particularly in the developing world, to support an exploding world population taking us from the current level of just over six billion to over nine and a half billion by 2050.

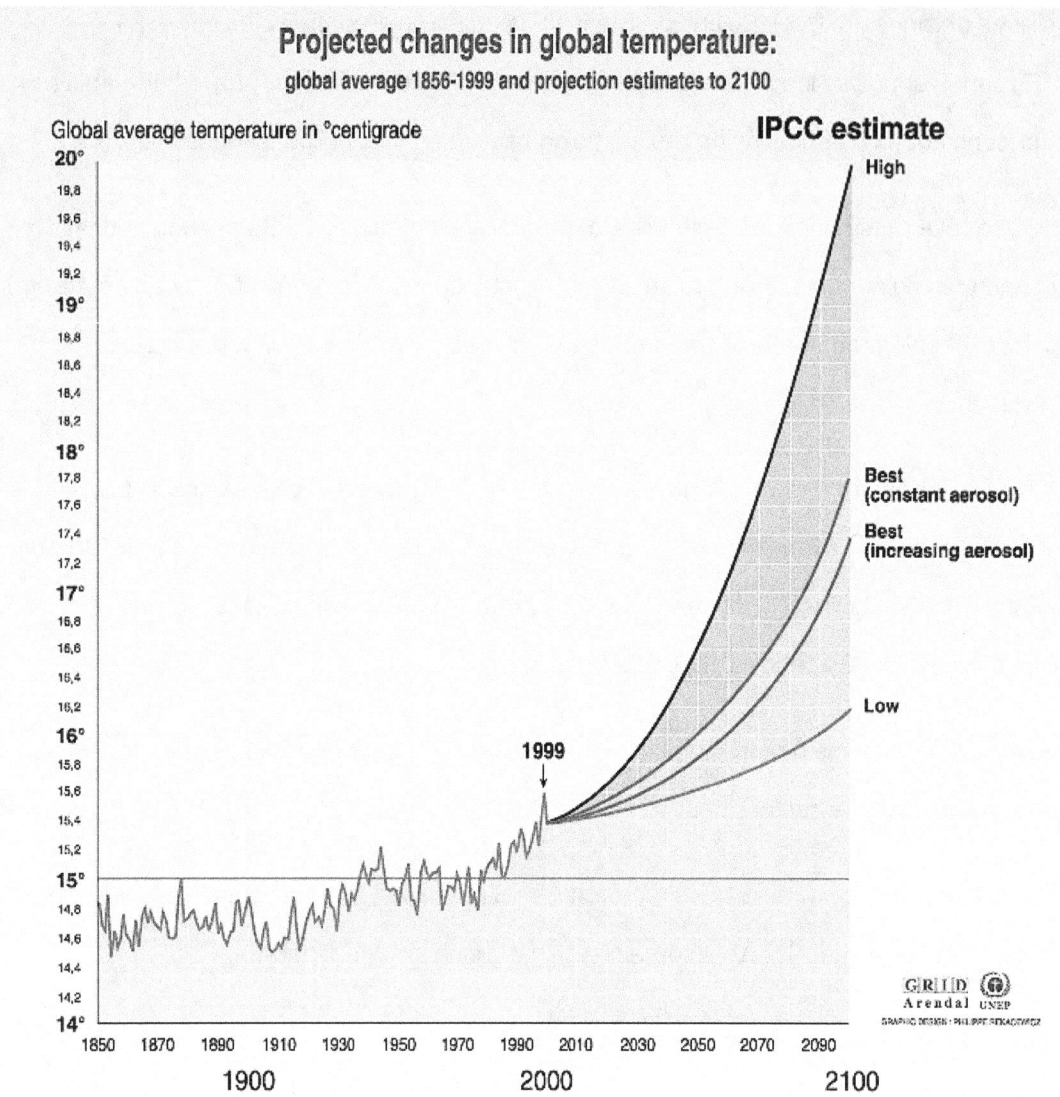

Projected changes in global temperature:
global average 1856-1999 and projection estimates to 2100

Global average temperature in °centigrade

IPCC estimate

High

Best
(constant aerosol)

Best
(increasing aerosol)

Low

1999

Source . Temperatures 1856 - 1999. Climatic Research Unit, University at East Anglia, Norwich UK. Projections: IPCC report 95.

Unchecked, temperature rises in the 5 to 10 degree levels would have devastating effects on weather patterns damaging the most vulnerable first; namely those who are already on the fringes of extreme latitudes in hot climates such as the developing world. Furthermore, flooding of some of the major cities in the world would ensue, such as London and New York, being caused by rising sea levels. Keep in mind; we know what happened historically when temperatures dropped. Going in the other direction, we can only surmise. But for extremes, we can build a good model.

Looking at what is causing such extreme rises in CO2 concentration; industrialised nations have to look at themselves first. Post industrial revolution, concentrations of CO2 have seen a marked rise, due to industrial growth being founded on fossil fuels - primarily in the early days coal - which supplied the energy to run: factories, homes, early transport and the heavy industries such as steel and iron.

Pressing on over two hundred years, the insatiable appetite for fossil fuels never abated across the northern hemisphere creating wealth, and greater participations in trade across the globe.

However, all the advances made and the creation of new sectors of industry for the development of man came at an unknown price as CO2 output was above and beyond its natural background production. And, beyond what the planet could absorb.

Man also started to remove the Earth's natural defences against CO2 by cutting down vast tracks of rainforest and other large areas of woodland to supply homes and industry so making the impact even greater. Some of that activity has still yet to be realised in the overall concentration figures.

With wealth, came rising populations further eating into resources; and forests being cut down to provide land for agricultural purposes. The methods used for removing forests has caused great damage to the atmosphere through slash and burn methodologies, releasing the stored carbon into the atmosphere.

By the second half of the twentieth century, scientists were beginning to observe the effects of Global Warming with changes being seen to the earth's climate, resources and the biodiversity.

It was noticed for example, our polar regions had begun to shrink. With warming temperatures, these great landmasses of ice were beginning to melt, fuelling an increase in warming. The ice sheets act as a large solar reflector. With a decrease in size, so a decrease in their effect, leading to more heat being absorbed into the oceans, so causing a greater melting effect.

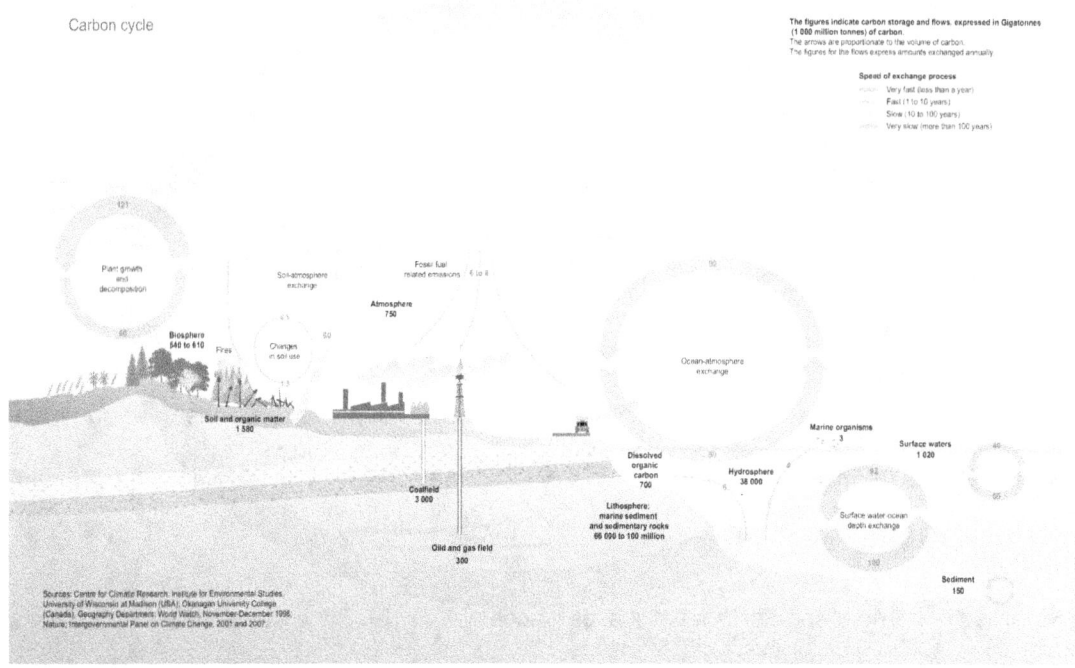

In short, the oceans warm, causing the ice to melt, and with warmer waters we have a rise in water vapour, which is very good at letting in solar radiation and retaining radiated heat from the surface, so once again adding to the global warming effect.

Melting of the great ice sheets is further accelerated by ice slipping from land- masses, such as the Western Greenland Ice Sheet. This slippage is caused by melt water flowing between the bedrock and the ice field and acting as a lubricant. As the ice weakens and is not being retained by the land - it fractures, and slips into the ocean. This in turn causes vast tracks of ice to melt causing rising sea levels.

Additionally, with warming ice sheets, so the tundra starts to thaw. The tundra has thousands of millions of tonnes of methane, trapped inside from tens of thousands of years of background emissions. As the tundra thaws, so this methane is being added to the current concentrations. What must be understood at this point is the CO2 levels that will arise from thawing tundra is greater than all the industrial nations combined.

It naturally follows, this chain reaction, unless abated and reversed, will continue to accelerate the GHG emissions and Climate Change taking man in to un- chartered territory of a 5 to 10 degree temperature rise by 2050 in the 'Business As Usual' scenario.

By 2050, the population will be over 9.3 billion people; yet, the potential for less useable land is huge. The temperature rise will cause devastating changes to weather patterns: hurricanes and tornados are already showing to be more frequent. High levels of rain fall over northern hemispheres, rising sea levels, vast flooding and more droughts in the hotter climates. The developing world will be worst hit due to their location.

If these warning signs continue to go unheeded, we are going to see greater displacement of people around the world, as flooding will cause the disappearance of well-populated areas of land. Many of the major cities of the world, both developed and developing are coastal, and will be destroyed by devastating flooding from rising sea levels. It means vast changes to the bio diversity of the planet: many animals, birds and reptiles will be driven to extinction. Many of our wonderful species are already extinct, or endangered creating a devastating loss to our planet.

Example: it is predicted under the Business As Usual scenario, that the sea levels will rise by at least one metre. To visualise this: if we allow it to happen, fifteen percent of Bangladesh will be flooded. This in turn will mean the displacement of thirteen million people.

Much educated and scientific debate is being conducted continually, but not as to whether it is happening, but as to how fast. Something needs to be done now to reduce CO2 emissions and stabilise CO2 concentrations. Business is one of the largest single emitters of greenhouse gases and as such, governments have started placing regulation on business, targeting emissions reduction and mitigation.

If everything is left un-checked, what the statistics means to Britain or mainland Europe, is the heat wave of 2003 will become a typical summer. It was a summer where over thirty thousand elderly and vulnerable people died.

We all have a coping range, and everything is designed around that coping range.

If the summer of 2003 was an extreme: what if that was now standard? Our coping range would have to move to current extremes, and new extremes will be beyond that. Therefore, we need to look at wide scale adaptation.

To help mitigate extremes, a strategy to reduce Global Warming impact is important. The location of efficiency and new technology energy production is not relevant, as any reduction, no matter where, benefits the planet as a whole. On this basis, it is important that all nations play a role; with the major industrialised countries being the main contributors to significant emission reduction through clean technologies and renewables.

Initial headline targets are set for 2012, with further target stages being set for the next forty years and beyond. Through constant scientific analysis the targets need to be constantly recalculated to take account of past emissions as impact becomes more evident as past emissions are added to current emissions.

As investment opportunities, product and service development opportunities and cost control opportunities become illuminated we can discuss the growth of the new markets, new technologies and delivery of profitable new projects.

China for example, has made strides to eliminating the most polluting factories, and replacing with modern and efficient one's: even though, China has now surpassed the US as the largest global polluter. But, if taken on a per head calculation, they are still deemed to be very low. China first made innovative decisions toward emission reduction when a twelve state report was compiled and found that if Climate Change continued unabated, then Global Warming would cause a ten percent reduction in China's agricultural output over the next 20 years.

Following Cancun, China can see the economic prize associated with a more advanced position in international climate change and is taking advanced steps of investment to reap the rewards.

Efficiency is going to be the main player: efficiency in energy and water usage, efficiency of new products and services and lowering waste: delivering cost reduction and meeting customer expectations through lowered risk and environmental impact.

Governments, in partnership with large utilities and emerging new players are developing more efficient ways of energy production and, diversifying sources of energy production such as renewables. Which, not only help in the fight of emission reduction but also develop new markets for energy production giving countries energy security to sustain development without an over reliance on current forms of supply which may be based on the importation of fossil fuels.

Cost saving and the business contribution

To start: producing too much carbon can be seen as inefficiency.

Sustainability and Climate Change is not an attack on business; however, it is a cultural shift – toward a more rewarding business.

Furthermore, to make Climate Change policies work, and create a sustainability strategy, it is important that the leadership is from the top. It has to be fully owned and understood from the leadership for it to be accepted, embraced and made to work for the business.

Business strategy needs to embrace sustainability as part of the core business to achieve greatest value. The development of a sustainability policy will deliver a comprehensive plan to increase energy efficiency and reduce environmental impact by developing continuous monitoring, reporting and communication of the sustainability performance as measured against the triple bottom line. The triple bottom line is - economic, social and environmental. All are going to play a major part in developing strength as a business and make that difference.

Four times as many large businesses engage in triple bottom line reporting than do small businesses. All indicators show this gap is only going to widen if SMEs do not embrace sustainability now. If we look at the European and US market, there are nearly fifty million small businesses, employing ninety seven percent of the working population in the private sector. That makes small businesses collectively the biggest business of all. We have already discussed that approximately one third of all Green House Gas Emissions are from business. That makes SMEs the largest constituent of those emissions; as yet, the poorest group to embrace sustainability.

Now is the time for SMEs to mould sustainability into all aspects of their business. SMEs have just the same opportunities as the large global companies towards sustainability. With the development of a strong strategy towards climate change and emission reduction any business is going to start saving money. Even if the savings are not immediate, they will very quickly soon surface on the economic bottom line. Notwithstanding the meeting of customer expectation, and improved market place attraction.

What are your emissions?

All businesses create emissions through daily activity: what needs determining is how the emissions impact the value of assets and operations.

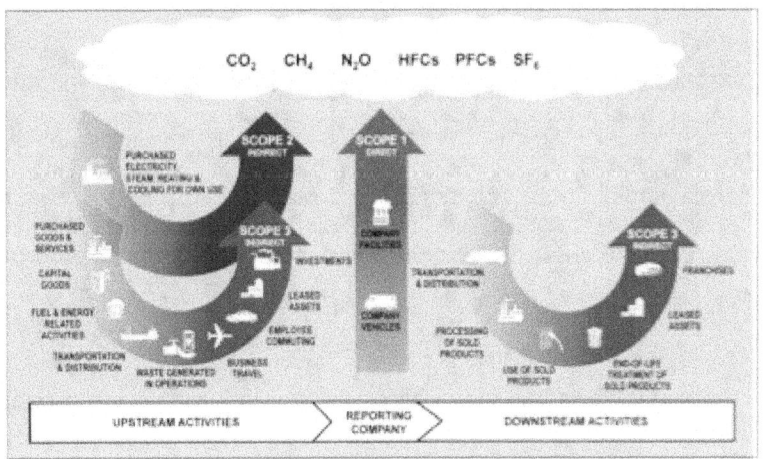

Greenhouse Gas Protocol Initiative © WRI & WBSD, 2011

Emissions are broken into several areas. Firstly, there are those that would be classed as direct. For example – fossil fuels a company actually burns, such as: fossil fuels for a central heating system.

Secondly, there are indirect emissions, for example: using electricity produced by a utility supplier. Lastly, there are scope 3 emissions, which are those emitted outside of the direct control of the company.

It is important to look at the business as a whole and beak it down into constituent functional areas. These make up the business as a whole. Each functional area generates emissions, which then create the whole.

Setting a strategy

Best strategies for a business are to make clear choices and the allocation of its resources, this being comprised of: ' *the steady accumulation of frameworks promising to unlock the secret of competition advantage*' – Walter Kiechel: The Lords of Strategy, Boston MA – Harvard Business School.

A sustainability strategy forces choices delivering clear actions, positive outcomes for the optimisation of resources.

This leads to environmental planning and strategic planning working together in understanding what the year ahead and future horizon looks like in terms of accountability life cycle as well as developing clear key performance indicators and budgets. Additionally, it protects the company from random environmental projects creating a sustained process with intended actions, clear outcomes, and business benefits.

By transcending the duality of environmental concerns and making money, an organisation exposes the false divide between environmental and business thinking.

Whilst business is not typically attuned to the feasibility and necessity of triple bottom line reporting: that of economic, environmental and social, the real truth of the matter lies in using considered environmental metrics with a commitment to work in a three dimensional way. With sustainability and overall corporate strategy linked, sustainability is given visibility, as it becomes part of the overall planning, budgeting and accountability processes. Thus, the business can operate successfully, and thrive, in an increasingly resource constrained world.

Whilst financial projections are important for allocating capital resources, and understanding trend analysis, when looking at adding corporate value, by creatively reallocating resources; effective implementers dismantle the internal barriers to corporate strategy implementation, see: Sustainability – a new business paradigm – Christopher Gleadle

Therefore, it is essential that managers should forge much stronger links between corporate strategy and other key management processes to ensure that strategy results in meaningful actions. And, if business leaders, whether large corporate, or importantly SME, are to overcome any biase towards immediate short-term solutions and switch to longer term thinking, then they will have made significant progress in adopting an attitude suited to the mitigation of increasingly complex and interdependent sustainability risks and developing a cycle of continuous improvement.

So, setting a sustainability strategy is a deliberate action to achieve deliberate outcomes – lower costs, drive innovation, team building, customer service, brand and reputation, sales and marketing, talent attraction, and competitive advantage. Thus, sustainability will help deliver the ability to beat the market.

It is important to understand sustainability addresses the three Cs of strategy – Competitors, Customers, Company.

Competitors - by driving innovation, meeting stakeholder expectation, and creating clear differentiation.

Customers – as pressure for meeting and delivering against sustainability issues transcends the supply chain, sustainability meets, and if correctly implemented, go beyond, customer expectation and improves service delivery.

Company – by reducing costs, improving team cohesion, talent attraction and driving innovation by removing the barriers to strategy implementation.

The deployment of a sustainability strategy also ensures verification of the actions to make outcomes provable in order to meet the strictest scrutiny, so adding the greatest value. This process of verification, by default, illustrates the interdependence of functional areas, and so expose and deliver greatest resource optimisation.

Furthermore, the market place is dependant on the state of the sum of previous events; therefore, to beat the market, your advantages need to be strong, robust and responsive in the face of on rushing market forces. Sustainability is poised to become the biggest economic game changer over the next twenty years.

So, ticking boxes, and playing along with the market, will expose a position, which is not as strong as it may appear. And, where as it may seem that smaller and weaker competitors as well as new market entrants are not deemed a threat; if they are taking a divergent strategy, one that embraces sustainability – verified, robust and embedded into the DNA – they will come through and be the winners tomorrow.

Because sustainability connects, and exposes, the interdependence of structure, conduct and performance, the company embracing sustainability will reap the rewards of positional advantage, by conferring and living by the unique benefits delivered to them. Many companies have to keep running just to stay in the same place – sustainability is a proven method that turns running into moving forward.

Sustainability, furthermore, breaks the cycle of typical strategy setting which applies to much emphasis on the status quo – metrics extrapolated from the last three or five years. Whilst, sustainability is about gathering the backward looking metrics; once turned to face forward, gives insight into cost reduction and process optimisation for the future.

And, whilst most trends emerge slowly, or very slowly, sustainability is gaining traction across the globe, as its implications are felt across entire value chains. Companies tend to react to trends, or in the case of sustainability, continue waiting for legislation. Leave it too late, and it will become almost impossible to mount a strategically effective response and will deliver no influence on shaping change to your advantage.

The cost of delay is steep, both in terms of operations as well as lost market position. Yet, for companies who have forged ahead on the curve have been able to tailor strategies to the new environment – and a great deal of economic research has shown – even through the recent recession – have taken a financial lead of competitors who have or still are ignoring the shifting market place.

For instance, companies that routinely go out of their way to experience the world from their customers' perspective routinely develop better strategies. Sustainability is a quality stakeholder engagement programme of continuous improvement. Once embedded into the DNA of the company, the whole team shares and aspires to the ethos; customers and suppliers become involved in the process and support the strategy. This does mean that decision makers must be taken on the journey of sustainability; create experiences which help them instinctively grasp the mis-matches that may exist between what the new strategy requires and the actions and behaviour that have brought success up to this point. By connecting the board, senior managers and employees, there is a support base for people with influence to feel connected to the strategy – as such; they may even become evangelists for it.

Whilst, strategy must be translated into an action plan, ultimately, when setting strategy, the three questions that need answering are:

1) Does it increase innovation?
2) Will it create value?
3) Is it material?

The answer is YES to all.

Get proof, speak to customers, speak to suppliers; but when setting strategy – make sure the insights and capabilities underlying them are real and not just the result of some carefully manipulated PowerPoint engineering.

It is easy to think success will just continue. The challenge is to watch for signs to the contrary and use those signs as the catalyst for change. Winning, like sustainability, is a journey and not a destination. It is a cycle of continual improvement, so be clear and understand where you are on your strategic journey as a business.

It is important to always be thinking about profitable growth, but you also need to be thinking about the value of risk. Sustainability strategy directly linked to company strategy underpins the very essence of strategic thinking.

Are you protecting your strongholds? Are you thinking about how your competitors are reacting? Are you thinking enough about how to create, and not just capture, value as the market matures? How much risk is there in your supply chain? How much will it cost not to develop a sustainability strategy?

Sustainability as a strategy is about optimising resource use and allocation and understanding what is working and what is not. Notwithstanding that, what does working really mean? Sustainability breaks down and modulises what is working so you can see what it actually looks like, what it means and what costs can be stripped out and processes optimised.

Sustainability is about collaboration, skills development, innovation and optimisation of the triple bottom line. Sustainability helps and guides to get specific about what you have the ability to shape, what points of influence you can begin to put in place – sustainability is invaluable.

Developing a sustainability plan

For a sustainability policy to be successful there must be buy in from the CEO and the board. Furthermore, success also depends on the engagement of staff, which delivers further rewards and increased value to the business.

Economic sustainability is the lifeblood of all business, and the sustainability plan gives visibility to the opportunities for reducing energy, water and waste and also acts as a catalyst for change and engages the staff into a perpetual process of continual improvement.

The plan starts with the establishment of the current status of sustainability, which involves identifying, and capturing the data and creating metrics by which the company is going to be environmentally valued.

Then by transforming the backward looking metrics into forward-looking tools a company can track and forecast liabilities.

The sustainability plan is a three dimensional process linked to the corporate strategy. This link gives visibility, as it becomes part of the overall planning, budgeting and accountability process. It delivers the balance between profit and the environment, through eco-efficiency and helps drive sales and create innovation, strengthening brand and reputation.

In maximising value, many completed studies have shown, the journey not only re-engages the staff in the processes of the business, but also improves team cohesion and motivation, lowers staff turnover and is a driver for attracting and retaining the best people.

Opening with a presentation on the process and what is required, demonstrate the purpose and goals; talk about what sustainability is and what it means to them as individuals and what it means to the company now, and in the future. Give examples of clients and suppliers who have already taken the sustainability route in order they can be involved straight away and that the staff can understand the positive impact of a sustainability plan.

Full involvement of management is essential through out, as this acts as a driver for full participation of the staff. It is not a process about just ticking boxes. Those who engage in that behaviour will not maximise the benefits and opportunities available.

To reduce bureaucracy and increase effective liaison across the company functions a sustainability champion should be nominated.

In small organisations this does not need to be a full time position and may be typically taken up by the MD. Within larger companies, the Health, Safety and Environmental Manager might typically take this role.

The sustainability team needs to embrace the full spectrum of the business and key roles would develop accordingly:

- Co-ordinator and team

- Start up and co-ordinating sustainability related activities

- Contribute and distribute internal sustainability documentation

- Consult with suppliers and customers

- Co-ordinate sustainability staff and deliver training

- Start to integrate policies and actions with staff, suppliers and customers

- Create partnerships to add value and commitment

Collaboration draws huge benefits so being inclusive gains much more commitment and it should be fun and keep all stakeholders informed as to progress at all times.

Understanding there is a difference between large and small companies; a guide to functional involvement is:

Board	Strategy, CSR, Sustainability
Finance	Create KPIs and financial performance of plan
HR	Incorporate sustainability into job descriptions, appraisals and induction literature
Procurement	Supplier sustainability performance and weighting
Legal advisors	Advice on correct wording into supplier contracts
Marketing	Develop a communication plan and incentives
Sales	Customer expectations and procurement criteria
H,S & E	Monitoring and Data collection
Production	KPIs, monitoring and reduction plan

Logistics   KPIs monitoring and reduction plan

Conduct a baseline assessment

From understanding the baseline, it is possible to see where reductions can be made in asset and operational efficiencies, cost savings and profit improvement. The company will gain an understanding of the risks to the triple bottom line: economic, environmental and social.

The three main steps are:

Identification of company (and supply chain) components

Identification of the impacts of company products and services

Identification of whole company impact

The baseline will allow your company to understand the value of the energy and environmental process across the organisation and its value chain. The process supports the continuous improvement and achievement of robust and meaningful reductions.

Therefore, in most cases the following will be included:

Buildings

Personnel employed (all offices, regions and countries)

Contracts with third parties

Vehicles

IT

Energy

Water

Travel

Commuting

Production

Services

Operations

As with any new processes, the initial task of data collection and verification is time consuming. However, once the new procedures are in place – and all involved personnel are fully aware of the actions; data gathering becomes routine, and part of normal operational procedure. Furthermore, with experience, companies find new information pathways opening up, and all sustainability information can be stored in one central location.

The emergence of environmental management software has simplified this process even further. As the data is gathered it can be input to one central repository. This enables the company to easily report on current situation and report on progress. All energy, waste and water streams – and ultimately supply chain - can be monitored and measured. Furthermore, with an understanding of the baseline, actions can be modeled and likely outcomes reported.

Having identified and quantified what it is the company emits, it is vital to understand the impact measured over a twelve-month period. Then on a rolling 12 month reporting cycle. This process sets the company against market expectations, delivers stakeholder involvement so further underpinning trust, brand and reputation. It also embeds the process of continuous improvement into the DNA of the business. By proving the case, and making written commitments, it ensures continuing success.

What differentiates sustainability from any other cost reduction initiatives is, it becomes part of the core of the business planning and processes. Aligning it to the corporate strategy gives it visibility and becomes part of the overall financial planning and budgeting cycle.

Research on earlier, inefficient, forms of cost reduction strategy confirmed: ' *only ten percent of cost reduction programmes show sustained results three years later.*' (Suzanne P Nimocks, Robert L Rosiello and Oliver Wright, "Managing Overhead Costs" mckinseyquarterley.com, May 2005.) Sustainability however, when embedded into large organisations, is the opposite, and has shown robust delivery and constant improvement over time supporting all value driven opportunities.

The application of methodologies or even technologies (IT solutions, Web, visual monitoring etc) and management practices impact on minimising the negative and maximising the positive.

Using current best practice standards can leverage suppliers to be graded and then certified by the purchasing company, for example: gold, silver, and bronze. The practices reviewed yearly and certificates supplied. This way, suppliers can be encouraged towards their own sustainability standards and incentivised to enter a cycle of continuous improvement. It must not be forgotten; the whole supply chain has to be included. If you are a supplier to a large company with sustainability embedded, they will or are now putting pressure on their tier 1 suppliers and expecting them to put pressure on their suppliers accordingly; as the supply chain is also a risk to the end company. Whilst traditionally the vision of what happens down stream has not been of importance, today, it is of great importance, as it affects the over all sustainability and foot print of end products and. services. Therefore, if a business unit has a supplier, who purchases components from a company in a developing country, and that company has poor social policies towards its employees, that is a risk to the business, and to the companies it supplies. Companies should be as aware of human rights abuses in the supply chain, as well as environmental risk. It is the business responsibility. In the internet age, bad publicity can spread quickly. The reputation and brand which years have been spent building, can be destroyed in the blink of an eye if suppliers are not vetted carefully, or get them to improve. Businesses are now getting another clear picture of the interdependency of all the processes that make up the whole. Get everyone on board – it is important.

Therefore the identification of a company's sustainability can be measured against:

% of employees engaged in sustainability methods

Sustainability mission statement

Sustainability position paper

Sustainability corporate policy

Internal management

% of printed materials on environmentally friendly paper

Use of green energy

Environmentally friendly commuting

Energy efficiency policy

Waste reduction policy

Water use reduction policy

Improvement in recycling and reduction in waste to landfill

Offset unavoidable emissions

Sustainability clause to contracts

Sustainable procurement

% of suppliers meeting standards and making commitment

Transport and distribution improvements e.g. vehicle choice, route planning etc

Don't forget to report every achievement – it has value.

Creating a policy

Create a framework for identifying, monitoring and improving the company environmental and social performance with a time horizon of, say, the next five years.

Internally

Goals among employees - % engaged, their role in development and implementation of the plan

Embed sustainability into the company DNA

Express into a single document

Externally

Express commitments to customers and suppliers [Position paper initially – give commitment]

Other stakeholders

Intention to reduce impact of products and services

Express how the company operates as a sustainable business

It is vital all senior management and directors of all operations support the policy. The policy being underwritten by the board motivates individual commitment to implement sustainable policies within the company and the supply chain.

Developing a policy

In order to encourage relevance and importance, consultations with a wide range of stakeholders should be undertaken including when possible, all staff and suppliers. In the first instance, establishing a concept text in the form of a position paper can do this. This can state the current position, a statement of intention, any achievements so far, and outline the methodology. In broad terms, state what the goals and aspirations are. This to be signed off by the CEO. An example paper might be:

The mitigation of climate change is a global challenge. [At Company A] we recognise that our operations, products and services have an impact on climate change and we aim to minimize this. As our business expands into new markets, we will manage any rise in carbon emissions.

We are [building on our early successes and] developing [further] climate strategies and carbon intensity targets in order to establish a more disciplined process and structure inside the company to manage our sustainability initiatives.

Our sustainability policy will deliver a comprehensive plan to increase energy efficiency and reduce our environmental impact by developing continuous monitoring, reporting and communication of our sustainability performance.

This process involves the communication and training of our staff in support of continuous improvement and the achievement of robust and meaningful reductions.

It is important our sustainability policy transcends our entire supply chain. This action allows us to be transparent to our customers by knowing the companies that supply us, with our goods and services are operating according to the same environmental standards.

The main areas of focus are:

1- Reduce emissions from our operations

2- Partner with suppliers and encourage them to reduce their emissions

3- Deliver products and services enabling our customers to reduce their environmental impact

If there are any initial achievements such as 14001 do not forget to include them in the opening statement for example: 'We have already made a commitment with our initial success of gaining ISO 14001, an internationally recognised standard for environmental management.' But do not lose sight of the fact; all statements must be provable and commitments adhered to - for their lies value.

Using standard practice for the establishing of a policy:

Don't start activities without a written policy

Understand the goals to ensure motivation

Goals and targets can be influenced from the carbon and environmental footprint and the mission statement

What are the objectives for the sustainability goals?

Targets must show the improvement made

All management to be engaged with implementation and monitoring

Keep flexible to enable any required modifications and allow for evolution over the long term

Communicate the intention that this is for the long term (constant cycle of improvement)

Keep ambition in check as setting targets too high can de-motivate

Engage suppliers and other stakeholders

Discuss the policy with a selected group of suppliers to gain their feedback and help to develop an effective policy that will then benefit everyone

A sustainability policy is a process and therefore all the goals do not have to be achieved at one time

Demonstrate improvements and always remember to report all successes

No matter how small it may be – communication is commitment – adds value to the business

The content of the policy must reflect the business processes including the lifecycle of all products and services including:

Internal management

Product management

Supply chain management

Partnership management

Customer relationship management

A sustainability policy in general should include:

Sign off from the board

Compliance to mission statement

Objectives as to the corporate policy

Address the issues raised in the environmental footprint (baseline assessment)

Relevant to the nature, scale and the impacts of the company activities

Be transparent

Work with current laws, regulations and any specific codes of conduct

Deliver the positive message of striving for continuous improvement

Cover all products and services

Aligned to the five key action areas

Engage all employees

Involve wider stakeholders and business partners

Reporting available to wider audience: via the web

Implementation of Action Plan

Whilst the sustainability policy has been given a time horizon of say five years, the action plan should be focused on smaller bite sized units. It is easier to reach targets within smaller time units and maintains motivation and commitment.

In developing the plan, a few areas to think about are:

Prioritisation of action areas

Setting objectives and targets

Define and structure responsibilities, budget and timeframe

The prioritising of action areas is the first step in a journey: a process of forced events, which has the long-term policy for sustainability in focus. All the goals cannot be achieved overnight – it allows the company to find out what does and does not work, for them. Not all companies are the same; therefore, setting the agenda is a bespoke piece of work, as copying someone else's plan will not achieve the desired impact.

This process allows for fine-tuning of the organisation and will highlight areas of inefficiencies in operations and allow for the cutting of waste, whether it is energy or water for example. It also brings to focus replicated tasks:

Therefore:

Highlight key areas from footprint assessment

High impact suppliers

Easy to reach targets at lowest or zero cost to achieve

Highest selling products and services by volume / value

Resource hungry whole life cost

Actions to be taken:

Environmental footprint results analysis

Policy objectives and set minimum criteria

Senior management approval of actions and tasks

Resources for running programme

Involve all departments and staff (barriers and silos removed)

Transparency

Keep stakeholders informed; gain their approval of objectives

Limit tasks to a realistic number

Consider capacity for supplier improvements

All actions and tasks should be SMART – Specific, Measurable, Achievable, Realistic, Time Bound

Keep records of all tasks and actions completed

Keep records for reasons for setting the priorities

Keep action plan brief and bulleted. Explanations can be appended

It naturally follows a timetable needs to be set, the responsibilities defined and budget agreed:

Decide on task sequence

Plan backwards from what needs to be achieved at the end of the year and what needs to be done to make that happen – what does success look like?

Who is responsible for each task and gain their input

In larger organisations there may need to be an action plan for each department / product / service

Management to be responsible for implementation or designated champions

Incorporate actions into company procedures and review progress and staff performance

Allocate budgets for each task if resources and materials required

Communicate action plan and expectations to stakeholders

In monitoring and evaluating the achievements the company demonstrates and reports the new found sustainability. It is much more than just ticking the box; but, as a process, becomes part of the company DNA, part of the overall budgeting and accounting of the business. By sustainability being part of operations and the financial process the result of the company sustainability policy is provable, measurable and meaningful. It therefore underpins trust and reputation.

The greatest results and achievements are made by breaking away from cost cutting and sustainability being operated on an activity by activity basis, and joined together by one coherent policy aligned to the overall corporate strategy. Over all strategy and sustainability are interdependent.

As part of the continuous process of improvement:

Have targets been reached?

What actions show little or no results?

What actions are needed to improve results?

Record all actions completed and future plans

Regular measurements

Which significant impacts have been addressed?

Actual performance against planned objectives

What worked and what did not?

Transparency

Adequate recommendations for next year

Benchmark achievements and new situation against customer expectations

Report results for all stakeholders

From the initial baseline measurements taken, and the then financial cost analysis, at the end of the first sustainability cycle; it is now possible, to record and report the achievements made, both in terms of environmental success, and cost savings made, when balanced against the business as usual model.

It is important now, that the yearly cycle of continuous improvement be reported. Commitments have been made to this effect in the initial position paper and first sustainability report. This commitment not only meets customer expectations, but also drives the internal engagement. This is a process and not a one off project, as it becomes embedded into the operations and financial analysis of the business.

Sustainability has to be part of the company DNA, and the DNA of all products and services to maximise value.

Sustainability performance is seen as an indicator of strong management, strong governance and long term thinking about future growth potential and risk mitigation and must be managed across all operations and the entire value chain.

Sustainable Procurement

It is important to speak with one voice. By suppliers making a commitment, it makes initiatives tangible – provable and meaningful – to maximise eco-efficiency reduce emissions and environmental impact through the supply chain, so reducing risk and improving value.

Sustainable procurement also links with the overall goals of the corporate sustainability policy, to reduce emissions and environmental impact both within its own organisational boundaries, and reduction of environmental impact on customers.

The supply chain measurement is part of the future and it is important to place in motion a method to understand, measure and monitor the impact of the supply chain: to quantify the supply chain impact as part of the overall footprint of the business.

This action is important as it meets with customer expectations now, and further enhances the trust and reputation of the company in the market place. Furthermore, by understanding now, and driving efficiencies, businesses set themselves apart from the competition and ideally help position themselves against future legislation.

Supply chains are typically an unknown quantity from a sustainability point of view. It is essential for companies to get an understanding of what environmental and social risks may lie un-seen. Additionally, what opportunities for Green House Gas reductions, improvements in costs through improved efficiency gains, transportation, customer use or product end-of life are available.

Start with a group of selected suppliers before taking it to a wider supplier base, and work out any programme inefficiencies.

To avoid confusion bring the selected group of suppliers to the table and clearly explain the business case behind the initiative and the expectations for their participation. By bringing the suppliers together in a collaborative way, everyone then has an opportunity to learn from one another.

Not all the suppliers will be novices: some may be further on the curve, which gives the initiating company the chance to learn from them. Furthermore, those who are already embracing sustainability will be delighted to showcase their improvements, and they in turn will motivate the others who have yet to start.

It is important to have a record of where you are starting from and where you want to go. If you want to help reduce your supplier's carbon and environmental footprint, you need to know what it is.

Green initiatives produce benefits for customers and suppliers. Customers will - as a minimum - enjoy fewer risks and a more responsible supply chain. Suppliers will strengthen their customer relationships through higher performance, and improve the cost structure of their businesses. Suppliers can also gain access to best practices and use that as a basis for innovation. With quick wins, a glimpse of future business value can be seen.

The economic return for any supplier willing to embrace the values of sustainability is in operational efficiencies and the achievement of cost savings. Cost savings will further free up capital for re-investment into new technologies

By building on a scorecard system, accountability is delivered to ensure the effort will produce results. The scorecard needs to layout clearly what the expectations are; provide clear sustainability goals, and what the results will mean to maintain a collaborative process for continuous improvement.

Sustainable procurement must cover all supplies, materials, ingredients, components, finished goods and services purchased to run operations and to develop, manufacture and deliver a company's own products and services. It naturally follows, this helps understand current practices, whilst developing and implementing the strategy for measuring suppliers' compliance with sustainable procurement goals.

Relationship and customer expectation compliance

Companies can work with hundreds – if not thousands - of suppliers around the world. With the diversity of suppliers sourcing in a global market; faulty components, toxic ingredients, unsafe working conditions – gross inefficiencies and waste can proliferate in such complex networks because, suppliers operate to their own individual practices and guidelines.

Effectively managing those relationships through a comprehensive sustainable procurement strategy can provide significant business advantages, such as: cost and efficiency improvements, better regulatory compliance, lower environmental impact and improved reputation with customers and other key stakeholders.

In addition, greater sustainability performance can enhance relationships with key stakeholders such as customers, investors, current and potential employees. For companies this can mean an opportunity to differentiate themselves from competitors, expand their access to new markets and tap new opportunities to grow revenue.

Ideally, a sustainable procurement policy should cover the following areas as a minimum:

Environment – Manage, monitor and reduce energy and water use. So reducing overall emissions and environmental impact. Increase re-cycling and lower waste to landfill, decrease any chemical use and improve efficiency.

Employment – ensure suppliers adhere to all applicable laws, rules and standards for labour practices:

such as UN Global Compact

Community – Ensure suppliers contribute to the communities they operate in.

Ethics and financial accountability – suppliers practice appropriate ethical trading standards, delivering transparency and operate to applicable accountancy standards.

Health & Safety – suppliers promote both safe working environments and safety in the products and services they promote.

Diversity – if possible promote diversity by allowing small companies as well as large company's to be part of the supply chain.

2 GREEN BUILDINGS AND SMART BUILDINGS

It is important to understand the interdependence between a green building and a smart building.

A green building is one that provides a healthy environment, a safe environment and a productive environment for its occupants. Whilst in association to those guiding principles, a smart building integrates the various systems, which when combined, allows the building to operate in a more energy efficient way.

The information fed back from the monitoring of the building processes allows analysts to make better decisions as to the planning and layout of the building, and make better use of the space available.

For example: in linking the environmental controls to security systems allows the environmental systems to know how many people are in a space at any one time thus delivering the right level of air conditioning. This eliminates the over-resourcing of the HVAC [Heating Ventilation Air Conditioning] system, so saving energy.

The St Regis Hotel in Shanghai linked twelve sub-systems within the building controls management system and saw a forty percent reduction in energy consumption.

In a recent report issued by Gartner, up to fifty percent of space is under used. Yet, all this space is still being lit and it is still being made to be environmentally acceptable for occupation: this energy is being wasted. Integration of lighting and the use of occupancy switches - lighting can be utilised only when it is needed.

Lighting

Lighting averages twenty six percent of primary energy in commercial buildings and yet how often do we see areas being lit where there are no people?

When lighting an area it is important to think through the use of the space and what the prime purpose of the lighting is going to be. It is very easy to look just at light switching, and move solely to new technologies of lighting and then receive the pay back over the calculated period of time after the investment has been made. However, looking at the lighting in a more holistic fashion from the outset can actually save money at the front end too.

For example: in a commercial building such as a head office where all the staff are sat at work stations; much of the floor space can be given over to walk ways and empty space between workstations, and these areas are lit from over head. Furthermore, the lighting for the workstations will also be supplied from over head. In effect this means that much of the light committed is being wasted.

A way around this situation is to think about what the priorities are. In pole position is the lighting needed for the people to do their job effectively. Then, when people are moving from one workspace to another, they can do so easily and in a safe manner.

To this end, task lighting on the workstations from desk-mounted lights can provide the adequate lighting needed for work. Using technologies such as LED lighting can provide the adequate lighting needed in an efficient manner whilst have a whole life of up to fifty thousand hours.

If the walkways are then lit either by LED or fluorescent lighting that washes the walls with back ground lighting, this solution can produce a calm and sympathetic work environment and using lighting that is much more specific for the job it has been employed to do. Such solutions can produce significant reductions in energy consumption, both through the new technology employed to deliver it, and the volume of lighting needed.

Another consideration to be thought through is: do you really need to replace all the lighting you have? Or, can you plan to only replace some of the lighting. Because, if you plan first, there may be an acceptable way of re-wiring a lighting circuit to employ only the ceiling lighting needed, which, would be a great deal more cost effective than a whole sale lighting replacement strategy.

Low energy and high quality are not incompatible and it is a matter of thinking through quality over quantity. With reduced glare and thought given to colour and distribution, a safe and comfortable environment can be created: one that is more conducive to delivering productivity through less stress related disorders that can often be associated with over lit, bright offices, using ceilings packed with fluorescent tubes. This action is conducive to following EU directives and health and safety executive policies for the introduction of less-hazard to health lighting.

So, task lighting and ambient lighting solutions can deliver cost savings in implementation, whole life running costs and produce a more productive work environment; a green environment.

Furthermore, if the lighting is linked to occupancy and movement, task specific lighting can also be switched on and off automatically so further reducing energy burn. We all believe we are only going to leave our desk for a minute or two, so we leave the lights on. More often than not, we are away from our desks much longer.

Be a master of your energy use - design technology in, not out. Don't just think to change the equipment, change the design. Isolate lighting on lighting circuits that is superfluous; build it into an over all management system that buildings' occupants control, and not the other way round.

Additionally, think about the natural light available in the offices and other workspaces. It is important to think about how the sun affects the building, and best natural light advantages. Think out redesigning the office or other workspace layout to take full advantage of natural light, which means switching off unnecessary artificial lighting for longer periods.

Is the best use being made from the orientation of the building? Is it possible to add some more windows? Once again, such simple changes do not only make a difference in the energy consumption of the building, but also to the overall environment in which everyone works, making the building more environmentally friendly, a more pleasant place to work, a green place to work.

Windows don't just provide access to natural light, but also add to the comfort of the building both in terms of well being for the occupants from a lighting point of view, but also give the opportunity for natural ventilation. Furthermore, up to date windows provide outstanding insulation for heat retention in winters, and heat reflection properties for summer temperatures, and also deliver excellent acoustic properties from outside interference.

If these changes are then linked to environmental management systems, then best use can be made of the systems you already have in place. By constant monitoring of the energy use, other changes can be prompted.

Energy Monitoring

At little or no expense if supported by the utilities, it can be cost effective to install energy meters for specific work areas. This can provide insight as to how the space is being utilised and mapped against key indicators such as production, weather, occupancy and space utilisation.

It is important to monitor the energy use month by month to provide the key metrics as to design and layout of work areas. The greater the volume of data gathered the better judgments that can be made as to changes that need to be introduced to deliver cost reduction and thus emissions reduction.

If the working environment is supported by air conditioning it is important to think about the heat load the building is being stressed by. Up to one third of heat load in a commercial building is due to electrical equipment and solar heat through windows (Franconi + Huang 1996 cited in Lee et al, 2002).

Reducing the heat generated through electrical equipment can be a combination of many simple things to create a big impact. For example:

Use software or automatic switches to switch off equipment when not in use – such as faxes, copiers and computers.

Replace any old cathode ray tube monitors with energy efficient LCD

Make sure procurement right size all new equipment for intended use

Reduce printer use – double side. Make black and white a de-fault

Encourage on-screen viewing of documents – avoid printing

Encourage staff to always switch off their computer

Reducing heat from lighting is combined with the initiatives to reduce the energy load for lighting, but has the double effect of also affecting the heat load on the air conditioning system. A brief list of possible actions to implement:

Replace existing florescent lights with T5

Use light reflectors to improve light efficiency

Install movement detectors

Use photo sensors that reduce the lighting load when there is sufficient natural light

Replace incandescent lighting

Zone lighting in offices with their own independent switches

High intensity or metal halide lighting for large areas

Use light colours or semi-reflective surfaces

Reduce the height of partitions between workspaces

IT and data centres

With the growth of capacity and larger and more powerful servers replacing smaller ones, in a growing organisation, the relationship between power and cooling can quickly get out of sync.

With Blade servers and the growth of virtualisation, proper optimisation of power and cooling in a high-density data centre environment will quickly show cost savings with reduced energy consumption.

As the virtualised environment grows to meet the business need, the power and cooling systems, if properly deployed, will support the deployment of the virtual environment.

The main benefit of virtualisation is the speed in positioning and scale of the environment. It is only natural to deploy power and cooling that meets the new challenges presented by a non-static data centre environment.

Therefore, the first thing to understand is the efficiency of the data centre. With that in mind, a collaboration which has developed very successfully over the last few years is Greengrid: this is a collaboration of over one hundred companies, who may be competitors in the business world, but have developed an effective union to develop and drive ever more efficient data centres and reduce the energy consumption and so dramatically lower emissions. This collaboration has developed internationally recognised standards for the recognition of sustainable and efficient data centres. The scales developed are: Power Usage Efficiency (PUE) and Data Centre Infrastructure Efficiency (DCiE). These standards being added to by recent innovations for the complete measurement of carbon (CUE) and water (WUE).

It is important to understand what these mean for any executive or procurement professional who is either in control of a data centre, or procurement professional that is buying in the services of a data centre for the managing of IT as a cloud* based solution.

* Cloud is internet based computing using resources within a remote data centre

PUE = Total facility Power / IT Equipment Power

Where a rating of one would be perfection. Therefore, it is the aim of all data centres to get a PUE rating as close to one as possible, and this standard has been adopted internationally as the benchmark of best practice.

Additionally, the reciprocal measurement DCiE is defined as:

1 / PUE = IT Equipment power / Total facility power X 100%

Total Facility Power: is measured from the meter. But, this reading could well be covering the use of an entire facility, such as offices, if the data centre is contained within a mixed-use building. Therefore, it would be advantageous to have the data centre metered separately to avoid complicated and approximated calculations.

IT Equipment Power: this is the power calculated to be delivered to the devices within the data centre which is used separately for the managing, processing, storage and routing of data. This would include: servers, storage devices, network components etc. This value is the output of all the distribution units in a data centre.

By using a calibrated measurement such as PUE, if changes are made it is possible to measure the impact of the change from an energy management perspective. Furthermore, it allows the actual power consumption to be understood of equipment that a company is looking to purchase.

For example: if a company is looking to purchase a server which has a consumption value of five hundred watts, and the PUE of the data centre has been calculated to be one point three, it follows, the power needed to be supplied is six hundred and fifty watts. Also, if the PUE were three, it would take one thousand five hundred watts to run the server.

As the PUE has become an international standard for a manufacturer of power efficiency services and equipment to measure and monitor energy use in this way to business users, PUE will add a great deal of support and value.

With this in mind, it is important to understand that the bulk of servers time is spent being idle and waiting for something to do; but, even at these times, the servers will be absorbing as much as thirty percent of the energy they consume at peak performance.

In a recent IDC report " Enterprise Class Virtualisation 2.0" as much as fifty percent of funds spent on servers is spent on power and cooling. Taking this into account, the total cost of ownership (TCO) can be as much as seventy percent of overall server budget.

Therefore, the move to virtualisation with the use of larger, more powerful servers, and removing the vast arrays of smaller less powerful servers, is a movement gaining traction around the globe.

The virtual environment also leads to a reduction in power and cooling. Yet, if the virtualisation move is not planned with the whole data centre infrastructure in mind, then the PUE will go up instead of down, as the facility will be over resourced in the needs for cooling and other services, as the load has dropped.

Virtualisation raises the opportunity to optimise the energy efficiency of the data centre:

Fewer servers are needed

Reduced load

However, PUE can increase if the support functions are not changed, and therefore, the fixed costs will limit the savings that virtualisation can offer. It follows, when planning the move to virtualisation, as stated before; it is wise to look at the whole infrastructure:

Update infrastructure support systems

Remove redundant or un-necessary equipment (cooling etc)

Switch to devices with lower parasitic drain

To maximise the cost savings virtualisation will bring, consolidate and reconfigure the power delivery. Additionally, consider the design and layout of the data centre and adjust the cooling infrastructure. This will improve return on investment of the change.

By re-visiting the design and layout of the data centre it is important also to understand the thermal characteristics of the data room. This can be done by monitoring temperature readings across the room and discover where hot spots are and address these issues accordingly.

By looking at hot isle /cold isle configurations and shifting the cooling units into the rows of server racks- the cooling can react to the changes and be delivered where it is needed; delivering short air path cooling.

At this stage, it is also important to understand what other risks may be present of the power and cooling being oversized for the new energy efficient technologies being deployed. These could range from temperatures falling below the recommended operational range of the cooling equipment and as such void warranties. There could be shorter compressor life due to repeated short cycling.

But by reducing the energy consumption, future demand also has to be allowed for, and therefore flexibility is key to avoid stranded capacity.

Stranded capacity is where there is one or two required resources but cannot access a third for successful deployment so leading to inefficiencies. Such examples of stranded capacity might be:

Oversized cooling at a location

Racks with power and space but insufficient cooling

Power and cooling but insufficient space

Therefore, to maximise the return on investment, it would be important when looking at any re-design of layout:

Change of density

Changing loads

Increased rate of change

Unforeseen changes

Interdependencies

Lean positioning

Efficiency should not be an after thought – design and the capabilities of the infrastructure can be tailored to the business needs, resulting in a cost efficient solution.

In terms of the overall sustainability of the business, and the aligning of data centre efficiency to the overall sustainability strategy, it is best to think of the design as building in eco-efficiency. In other words, optimise architecture to meet current and future needs without over committing or under resourcing.

When planning the reduction of power consumption, it is important to design out over sizing and right size the physical infrastructure. Looking at more efficient air conditioning and investing in more efficient power delivery equipment and virtual servers help this process.

Implementing improved data centre cooling architecture can be developed with in-expensive solutions to improve cooling efficiency. By standardising the power delivery systems also assists in understanding the economic benefits and the savings to be derived from the change expressed in term of: savings / KWh = £ / KWh. Therefore, power consumption becomes an integral part of the design strategy.

As data centre efficiency should be linked to the overall corporate sustainability plan, it is important to embed the PUE into that plan; establishing the current status, by identifying and capturing the data and creating the metrics by which the company is going to be environmentally assessed. Then, through careful planning, the backward metrics can be transformed into forward looking tools to track and forecast liabilities. And, because the sustainability plan is delivered as a three-dimensional process linked to corporate strategy, this link gives visibility, as it becomes part of the overall planning, budgeting and accountability process.

Hence, it is important, that within data centre planning, the plan must be expressed in the same language of overall corporate planning.

It makes sense to bridge the gap between environment and financial well being, and the gap between corporate strategy and IT; understanding, IT needs to be part of the strategy process, to deliver and support the vision and the goals. This way, IT can take a more modular approach to new systems and infrastructure, and avoid over sizing with too much power and too much cooling, but deploy resources inline with plan achievements.

After all, research has shown that a typical data centre is built to support three hundred percent of requested power and cooling capacity. This results in higher than needed up front costs and higher maintenance costs.

So, in reducing power consumption, other factors need to be built into the new plan, covering questions such as: what does the power cost in £ / KWh? This way, when planning for efficiency you can start to calculate the return on investment. Not forgetting that energy prices are going in one direction only, and that is upward. So build in a sensible scale over the determined plan implementation time. As with constant monitoring of the energy use to make choice decisions more informed, so monitor energy cost, and apply against the agreed metrics.

From the overall corporate strategy it is important for IT to understand how the business is planning for customer change and market change, as this will have an overall impact on futures and therefore affect distribution. These futures will all affect: demand, use, peak, seasonal etc. Understand; just because cost is seen as a moving target, it does not mean businesses have to pay an unknown amount each year. Waste is expensive!

As we have said earlier, research has shown that less than half the power going in to running a data centre is used to run the actual IT load.

Vendors of equipment need to provide information on energy consumption across a range of conditions. And procurement, as part of a 'Sustainable Procurement Policy', should be insisting on such metrics in order to be able to make better informed choices with regard total cost of ownership (TCO).

Reducing energy requirement of IT load is the easiest to apply. For example, a data centre could:

Replace legacy servers with dual or quad core servers

N way servers using single core be replaced with multiple core CPUs

Blade servers – different processor configurations so can tailor to applications – much more energy efficient

Enterprise hard drives – higher capacity – better performance – no increase in consumption

Virtualisation – fewer physical servers

The major consumers of energy remain:

Switchgear

UPSs

PDUs

Transformers

Air conditioners

Humidifiers

Cooling pumps

Heat – rejection equipment such as chillers and towers

Over-sizing and poor insulation and poor airflow control leads to waste: and waste = money.

Rightsizing is critical to maximise efficiency as studies have shown, with savings up to thirty percent. It follows; it is not just about buying what is advertised as the most efficient, because, it is no good if the whole design does not maximise best use. This can be illustrated by humidity in a data room – too little and you get static build up, and too much you get moisture. The balance has to be right.

Planning

Understanding the business as usual metrics gives the baseline to measure change, and allows you to forecast and create exception reports. For those using environmental management software for managing and reporting the overall sustainability policy this is made simple. And, the exercise allows the data centre to understand what percentage of the current total power and cooling is utilised. What new technology would have a negative impact and how would new equipment affect safety margins.

Furthermore, when making change it is also important to think about what redundancy is going to take place with the implementation of new primary equipment. And, such new equipment: how does this affect the cooling model? How much growth will the current or planned infrastructure support, and how does that fit in with the overall corporate strategy and growth plan? Not forgetting to relate this to the planned customer or predicted market place change. Where is the optimal location of the new equipment?

With so many variables infiltrating into the planned model for change, it clearly shows, data centre efficiency is once again showing it clearly follows overall sustainability planning and strategy, as it has to be, and is, a holistic process. And, like a sustainability strategy, it is introducing a Life Cycle Analysis for the IT support function as it is important to understand the TCO as well as the planned IT load.

In order to build against futures and maintain right size to maximise on efficiencies, it could be better to standardise on modular and flexible power and cooling systems and possibly look at hybrid cooling architectures so rightsizing power and cooling equipment.

By constantly monitoring what is happening inside the data centre, with change from your baseline, the metrics compiled will give a clear picture as to where the plan is not working, keeping in mind – 1 watt of power requires 1 watt of cooling.

Cooling equipment also has heat rejection equipment (in small facilities these two functions may be conducted within the same unit). So, cooling and heat rejection must be evenly matched using the lowest rated component for making the capacity calculations.

Because we have now moved to the importance of avoiding demand fighting, all systems within a defined area have to be of the same mode. For example, it is not practical to have components next to one another, where one needs humidity and the other needs to de-humidify. That just leads to waste. Once again, studies have shown that there are savings to be made of up to thirty percent by addressing demand fighting.

It naturally follows; avoid short cycling through checking the airflow and checking filters on a regular basis as part of routine maintenance. And, by regular monitoring of temperatures, it is easy to determine if there are any areas where the temperature is outside of the defined range, which can lead to a reduction of system performance, and a reduction of life span, leading to unexpected shutdowns of equipment.

Managing airflow is important to reducing costs as the equipment runs at optimal temperatures. This can be managed with things as simple as using blanking plates in order that warm air is not drawn back down into the rack. Furthermore, simple things like checking the placement of vents and tiles – for example: have they been reconfigured since the equipment has been changed?

The importance of correct free flow of air cannot be understated as a cost effective method to reducing costs, and correct air containment. Keeping the right air in the right place. The common methods: Cold Air Containment (CACS) and Hot Air Containment (HACS).

The three main areas to consider for cooling are:

Room cooling: re-configure new equipment on the floor

Row cooling: no need for raised floor – CRAC contains air and reduces the energy needed

Rack cooling: most flexible method by cooling what you want when you want it. This method deployed using rack mounted cooling.

Hot isles / Cold isles

Constantly rising energy costs combined with rising data centre energy consumption have together created the need to look at – and understand – more efficient cooling technologies and strategies.

Many data centres still rely on perimeter cooling with raised floors allowing hot and cold air to mix, therefore focusing the need to separate the hot and cold air to help lower costs. Currently, the methodology for air separation is the change to cold aisle containment (CACS) and hot aisle containment (HACS).

With perimeter cooling using cold room air conditioner (CRAC) units, the raised floor is used to deliver the cold air to the source points of heat. Hot air then mixes with cold air and returns to the CRAC units via the return vents. Typically, the rack rows have not been set up in consistent rows, and as part of a past risk mitigation strategy, there is over sized power consumption through the cooling components, so reducing efficiency. Over-sizing was seen as risk mitigation to avoid capacity shortage and minimise any downtime.

In the past, overheads were relatively low through energy costs and therefore it was not seen as a priority to develop a strategy for energy conservation.

Therefore: by having row based cooling and separating hot and cold air, energy is reduced by not having to force air – over what sometimes could be long distances – under the floor, with all the obstructions that would entail.

With hot air being captured and removed at the source point of heat, this in turn also reduces risk of humidity build up, leading to humidifiers running for less time – saving energy and water.

The methodologies being identified enable right sizing, so further reducing energy consumption: and saving money.

Data Centers in short

We must not forget that no two data centers are alike. The ideas in this book are not designed to be exhaustive and can apply equally to a large purpose built data centers as to one that is contained with in a multi-purpose building. The principles can just as easily apply too much smaller, cabinet contained racks, within an office for much smaller needs. The power needed to run IT systems is high, and following simple maintenance can reduce costs.

One key way to reduce costs is to create and maintain an energy efficient facility. But, this need not be complicated and not all solutions need to have a high front end cost – remember simple things like blanking plates – those small pieces of plastic that stop hot air being drawn back.

The starting place is understanding the current situation – the baseline – and then, identify the clear actions to deliver positive outcomes. Not forgetting, sustainability in an organization is a fantastic catalyst for change and collaboration. Learning from others and sharing ideas will deliver much progress.

As we have discussed, it is important to link green IT to the overall sustainability plan, as the combined efforts of moving away from activity – by - activity projects, will improve the company's overall bottom line as well as improve operational efficiency. After all, IT is a mission-critical part of any modern company, and it needs to be fully embedded in all corporate strategy.

Managers at all levels within in an organisation want to drive energy efficiencies, particularly bearing in mind, that many companies are beginning to link sustainability achievements to annual bonuses. This makes efficiency very personal.

Within the IT space, virtualization is a great way forward to drive down energy consumption as multiples of racks can be reduced down to one server. But, do not forget to rescale the support services such as cooling; otherwise, there will be over resourcing, and not maximizing on the energy efficiencies. Improve the total cost of ownership, and save money.

Sustainability – Green IT – is a global issue and not one for just a few. It needs to be made part of core business practice, part of overall planning, accountability and strategy. Give it the visibility and achieve success.

CACS

This system of cooling is used in traditional data centre environments; but instead of using the whole room to deliver cold air under the floor, the cold air is contained inside the aisle with the hot air being emitted into the room and so separating the hot air from the cold.

The contained aisles can have roofs and doors at either end and therefore the cold air is emitted in close proximity to the heat source and therefore reducing the energy consumed. With careful planning and design, higher rack densities can be achieved with a row based solution, and removes the need for cold air being pumped under the floor space or using floor based fans to improve the airflow. Therefore, the need for raised floors can be eliminated. Yet, the downside to this solution is if there were a power failure to the cooling, the temperature inside the aisle can rise rapidly leading to a failure.

All of the cold isles inside a data centre must be contained so eliminating any hot/cold air mix. As the hot air is expelled from the isles into the room, this can make the working environment un-usually warm. To avoid the staff believing, that due to the warmth of the room, there is an impending failure, a behaviour change needs to be instilled. Furthermore, by installing temperature sensors within the isles, then the working temperatures of the racks can be visually monitored to ensure compliance with operating standards.

Additionally, any other equipment, such as stand-alone systems, fire equipment or lighting, will need to be assessed as to their operating protocols. However, this situation can also be seen as an opportunity for further energy supply efficiencies through hot air extraction to other parts of the building for heating offices or other buildings – making the data centre a further potential resource.

HACS

This system contains the hot air, and cools it for the equipment air intakes ensuring efficient air distribution and separating the air supply from the return paths. Hot isles are currently seen as one of the best scenarios away from the traditional computer room. Doors at either end of the rows, and the roof containing hot air for in-row cooling with variable speed fans and temperature controlled air supply to the cold aisle.

This allows for maintaining higher temperatures; and the HACS environment moves slightly more air, drawing on room air; thus, giving a slight reduction in return air temperature to the cooling units, which leads to more efficient running of the cooling units and better energy efficiency.

As with either solution, it is important to understand the equipment operating standards and the return temperatures they can handle. For example: higher room temperatures give better heat exchange across the cooling coil giving higher efficiency.

Whilst hot isles operate at around 100° F with high-density servers is typical: with cold isle – the whole room is maintained at 100° F to achieve the same level of efficiency. Therefore, with HACS, there is not the impact on the surrounding room temperature and the room can be set at operating to 75° F. With CACS, the room temperature will rise as the hot exhaust air mixes with room air outside the cold isle on its way to the air intakes of the cooling systems. The hot air from the HACS is contained inside the isle away from the room; therefore the existing cooling systems are not affected.

HACS can be deployed with no changes to the current cooling systems unless there is a need to reduce the current cooling configuration, eliminating over-sizing, if there is a move to virtual servers so reducing the quantity of servers available.

Therefore

By preventing the mix of hot air and cold air leads to efficiency. To achieve this, HACS is more efficient than CACS as it allows for the channeling of hot air direct to the coolers. However, this does mean a greater deployment of ducting through the ceiling, but allows for a more comfortable working environment. And, HACS is more easily deployed anywhere in a computer room.

Additionally, HACS can draw on room air in the situation of a cooling system failure allowing more time for a calmer shut down or more time to allow for the operation of back up systems.

Both HACS and CACS have a superior power density and efficiency compared to traditional cooling architecture. CACS offers some improvement in perimeter cooling layout but HACS is more efficient with row based design so delivering greater flexibility and address higher density IT requirements without having to increase data centre temperatures. It is the extra room heat which could affect un- contained space; which, certainly for some owners / operators, where the line is drawn for no to CACS.

It is on this basis where we find from many studies, that most high density data centres - whether new design or retro fit - incorporate some form of HACS

Water Management

As we take this journey together into the world of the sustainable business, it cannot be emphasized more strongly, that all facets of a business need to be encompassed by an appropriate sustainability policy. As we have discussed before, sustainability acts as a catalyst for change – it also acts as a new lens to view the business by. It shows the interdependencies of all the processes and systems that make an efficient business. It shows how these interdependencies react with one another causing cost. The opportunity is to better understand these interdependencies and realise the opportunity for driving down cost and making a positive effect on the environment.

The management of water use can have a very positive effect on a business. With correct monitoring, management and reduction there can be significant savings improving the economic bottom line. Reduction also brings a positive effect of the environmental bottom line and secures an important part in positive sustainability reporting to underpin brand and reputation.

Use less water = pay less for water. However, there are other parts of the story, which relate to water. For example: using less hot water leads in turn to lower energy bills. Less wastewater leads to lower bills for treatment.

As water and energy costs rise, the return on water saving initiatives deliver better returns on investment making the business more competitive. But not all initiatives need to be expensive. Some are very simple. Kimberley Clark Smart Flush. A bag which can be hung in the water tank of a toilet, which, when it has absorbed water and expanded to its full operating size, will reduce the flush of the average toilet by one litre. This could equate to a saving up to two thousand gallons a year, per toilet.

Best performance can be measured against simple things: fixing leaks, improve the efficiency of the amenities so reduce water.

As with energy, effective water management starts at understanding the base line. Where the business is now. How much the business spends on water and aligned services every year and so how much it consumes. It is important to take these figures and create simple key performance indicators, such as, how much water you consume per square meter, or by staff headcount. These baseline metrics, like with energy, are going to give you the ability to understand where waste is, what reductions can be made and make the reductions meaningful as part of the sustainability cycle of constant improvement.

Adding sub-meters is a good way to understand water consumption of different areas of a business. How much production uses, the offices, warehousing etc. The readings taken from sub-meters will deliver a good snapshot of water consumption across the business.

Remember: cost of water = metered water + costs of sewage and wastewater + hot water.

Water loss from a business can occur in many areas, some which will not have any visibility. For example: if the business has an office environment controlled by an HVAC (Heating, Ventilation and Air Conditioning) system. Water loss can be due to leaks in the system or excessive water use due to the system being oversized or excessive operation.

Water loss can occur if the HVAC system uses cavities instead of sealed ductwork. Temperatures are too high or too low. Poor maintenance and cleaning causes the system to run inefficiently.

Heat from excessive lighting and heat from electrical equipment warms the air causing the HVAC system to run excessively. Furthermore, less efficient electrical equipment causes more heat. Heat from electrical equipment left switched on when not being used, or being left on stand-by causes higher energy consumption, but also higher water consumption. As can waste heat from product displays or ineffective building entrances.

The amenities can be a very large drain on water: toilet leaks or poor seals on urinals, broken valves and excessive flow rates from taps (hot and cold). So, any ageing amenities leads to wasted water, wasted energy and excessive labour costs in their maintenance.

It is also important to consider the hot water system from the perspective of: is the temperature too high causing people to use cool water in sinks to cool it down? Does the hot water system have leaks? Are there inefficient dishwashers? This all leads to excessive water use, wasted energy and too much chemical use.

The interdependencies of systems within a modern business show how they all react on one another to cause waste, but deliver the opportunity to save money.

Managing water must be part of the overall sustainability policy, as water management needs to have senior management support, signed and supported from the CEO. This gives water visibility, as there is a relationship between energy consumption and water consumption.

Management must take the lead and set the example for all others to follow. However, it is important to nominate a responsible person to monitor water management. As discussed in employee's engagement, it could very well be the sustainability champion. In many cases this will be the Health Safety and Environment Manager; as on a daily basis, they have their hands on the pulse of the sustainability policy.

From adding sub-meters, the business gains insight as to where the water is used. By constant monitoring and auditing the business can identify reduction opportunities. More than this, the business can identify and quantify the extra hidden costs of water. Reduction in water can lead to a reduction in electricity, gas, labour and chemicals. Furthermore, through constant monitoring, the identification of water using redundant equipment can also be made.

In identifying reduction opportunities it is not just the big things that can make a difference, but the small ones too. For example: reducing the flushing of toilets by a litre can show huge savings over a year. So, it is important to engage all the staff into thinking responsibly about water use and consider water saving ideas.

As with the corporate sustainability policy; it is important to involve all staff in the awareness of saving water, and to set realistic targets for water use reduction in order everyone can measure the gains, and measure the targets, against the agreed key performance indicators, such as use per square meter or use per member of staff.

With the development of water use reduction targets, a strategy needs to be defined on how to achieve the targets. This would fall into several areas:

Avoid water use - where possible

Reduce – where water use cannot be avoided – use less – remove leaks – regular maintenance programme

Re-use – can the water be used more than once?

Re-cycle – treated waste water from another process

Involving employees and fostering understanding, will promote a behavioral change. To facilitate the behavioral change, awareness will need to be raised to catalyse the thinking processes of employee's actions. Awareness can be raised through signage, emails, department meetings etc. Creating a competition for ideas can incentivise and motivate change. It helps the business and helps the environment.

The path to water reduction involves:

Leadership and demonstrated corporate commitment

Understand water use performance and opportunities

Plan to use water targets – define KPIs

Identify key personnel with water responsibilities and accountability

Improve operational and maintenance practices

Understand water and waste water regulatory requirements

Incorporate water into financial management

Technology and innovation

Measurement, verification and reporting

The corporate sustainability policy operates as a cycle of continuous improvement. So, water management should operate in an identical manner as a subset:

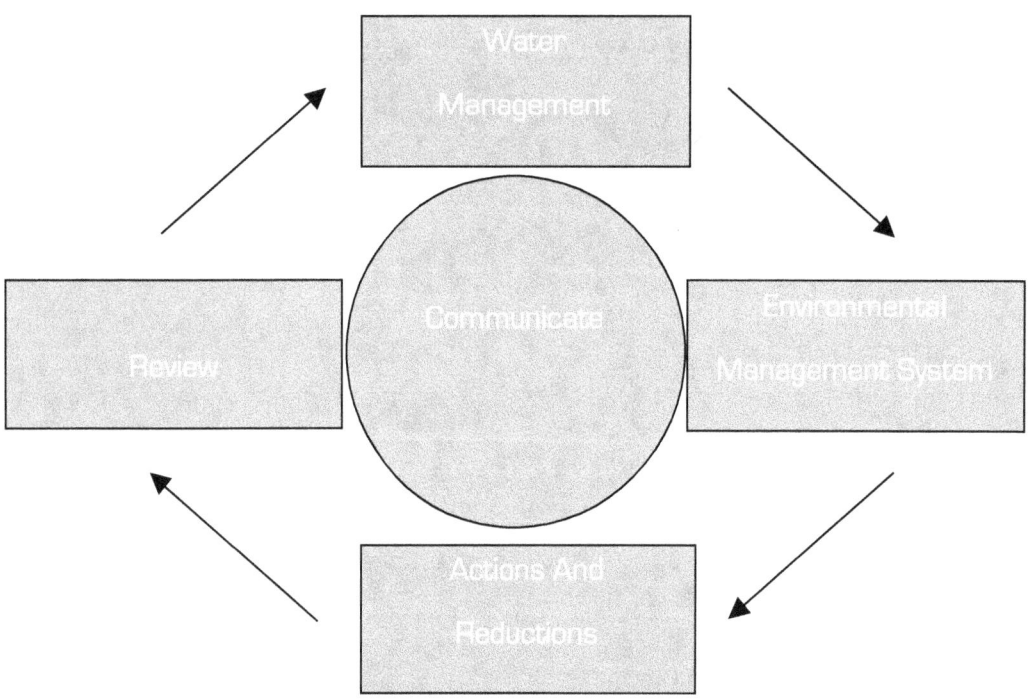

Sub meters applied to different systems delivers understanding of where and how water is used:

Cold water supply – different areas of the business. And where water is pumped to tanks for use – compare the outflow to the main meter readings. This will reveal any leaks in the system

Hot water supply – reduce temperature, prevent waste and leaks so saving water and energy

Amenities – toilets and urinals should be checked for leaks with improved maintenance and cleaning practices

Cooling towers – should your business have a cooling tower then meter the water in and through the bleed line.

Restaurants – Check the use of water against meals served and then you can benchmark for leaks and inefficiencies

Outdoors – irrigation systems and water features need to be monitored as leaks outdoors can be easily missed.

Shops – they may be part of a larger complex and water charges will be passed on, incentivising for water reduction.

Sewer discharge – checking the water in and the water out indicating the level of waste through leaks or evaporation

There are various ways of constantly monitoring water usage within the business: firstly there is manual checking. This is best done at the end of each day and the beginning of the next where there are no operations over night. If a difference shows up, and is significant, it is simple to register an issue, source and deal with quickly.

Automatic readers make this process continuous, saving time and display use patterns drawing the attention of the water champion to any un-usual water use. This process can be conducted via the internet, where data loggers are attached to nominated meters. The constant flow of information can be accessed via the internet, and emails or sms messages can be set for clients, if a dramatic change to water flow should occur from the base flow. This enables the people concerned to identify problems as soon as they occur.

If this is linked to an overall Environmental Management System, or Building Management System, the constant monitoring of water can be linked to other sub systems to compare water usage with occupancy or production for example.

With all the data logging and targets for continuous improvement, it is important to regularly review progress in order to define how much water has been saved and convert this metric as savings made against KPIs. This allows the financial department to quantify the costs and benefits of actions taken, and delivers understanding of the successes and failures – what worked and what did not.

With careful logging of water use information, we again discover the interdendencies of processes that make up a business. Another consideration is contract cleaning: therefore procurement needs to be fully aware of the sustainability policy and the drive for water efficiency. In this way, the use of water also needs to be included within sustainable procurement when tendering for contract cleaners for example. It needs to be understood as to what procedures contractors have in place for containment of water use. This can make a difference in the whole life cost of a contract. In other words, just because someone's tender is less; it does not mean they are cheaper.

How to reduce water use?

This book has always been about guiding and inspiring to make business more sustainable. It is not designed to make a CEO or other executives passionate about sustainability and climate change but to show how making a business sustainable supports the passions they do have. There is a solid business case for sustainability: it makes a business more competitive, more effective and more efficient. Sustainability promotes an extra dimension to the good governance of a business by demonstrating the executives have sight of long-term risks, and are embedding plans and actions to support risk mitigation and drive down costs. Through these actions, the executives are supporting and extending their brand and reputation and supporting the sales function to win business, and in many cases, giving their sales departments the ability to enter new markets through innovation and market attraction.

Water reduction is part of that process. Water reduction is about reducing costs to the business, and even small efforts can have big results.

It has been reported that as much as twenty five to thirty three percent of water in office buildings is used in the amenities.

Often, the flow rate of water from taps is much higher than needed in sinks for example, and by the placement of flow restrictors and reducing the flow, can show dramatic cuts in water use. The installation of sensor-controlled taps can ensure taps do not get left on after use.

Toilets use a great deal of water, and by either installing dual flush, or other solutions, such as expanding bags suspended in the water tanks, can reduce the amount of water used. Simple solutions that can show a pay back very quickly.

Placing sensors on urinals to make sure they only flush when they need to, and checking constantly for leaks, as part of routine maintenance, are also easy places to start.

Communication to all staff is important to incite a behavioral change and develop a new mind set for saving water.

To give an example: in a major city office building, over a six month period, water use went up by a staggering two hundred and thirty percent. Yet, there was no obvious change in the buildings use or occupancy. After a thorough inspection by the facilities manager, it was found that eight urinals were constantly flushing due to failing solenoid valves, which were then failing to close. This was remedied.

During the previous six months when the urinals were faulty, the extra water charge for the leak was $60,000. This is scaleable to your own business. The point being made: if there were constant monitoring, the rise in water consumption would have been seen straight away and could have been dealt with, saving such a large amount of money. This also illustrates the point – even though sensors are put in, it needs to be conducted with regular maintenance. Just installing part of the answer does not reap the greatest rewards. From an environmental point of view: had the failed solenoids been seen straight away, sixteen thousand-kilo litres of water would have been saved.

Looking on a more positive example: a twenty eight-storey office block, which on the ground floor has some tenanted shops and a café, under went a refurbishment of the amenities. In short, the basin taps had flow restrictors installed, reducing flow from twenty litres a minute to two. Furthermore, the kitchen sink and some showers had the same appliances fitted. The building was checked and was free from leaks. With no recorded change in building use or occupancy, water consumption fell by forty five percent. If your business could reduce its water bill by forty five percent – how much is that? Small things – big impact.

Landscaping

Water use in landscaping is related to the size of area that needs irrigating. Furthermore, the water holding capacity of the soil and the rate of loss through evaporation, soil infiltration and plant transpiration also affects water use.

The soil quality can be improved by adding organic matter (manure). With sandy soils, adding organic matter will help bind the particles together and so improve the ability to store water. With clay soils, the particles will separate, allowing better water infiltration. Whilst mulching slows evaporation down and so helps stabilize the soil temperature.

Plant choice and placing can also affect water use: group plants of similar water needs together and do not use plants native to rainforests or water based areas.

For grassed areas, try to make sure the soil depth is at least fifteen centimeters allowing deep-rooted varieties of grass to be used. Do not have the grass cut too short, as longer grass helps shade the soil so reducing evaporation. When the grass has been cut, during dry periods, leave the clippings as this helps keep moisture in the soil and also releases nutrients back.

If irrigation systems are used, they can be switched automatically to react to soil moisture, so reducing the risk of watering when not absolutely necessary, and stops over watering.

Collect rainwater for the use of watering outdoor spaces. And, if you are fortunate to have a roof garden, then this solution not only gives an excellent outdoor space, but also reduces dramatically the cooling load for the building, and adds excellent insulation for the winter.

Rainwater, if it can be collected, is good to use for water features as well as garden irrigation, and outdoor cleaning. But can also be used for toilet flushing. However, if being used for toilets, and this needs supporting by mains water, install back flow precautions.

Grey water: this is the water already used in sinks or kitchens but professional advice must be taken as to the treatment and applications.

3 COMMUNICATION

Sustainability reporting is an important ingredient to a successful policy. But for many companies, how to report and what to report is not straightforward. However, with the careful implementation of the sustainability policy, by the time a company reaches the reporting platform, much of the hard work has been completed; with the baseline measurements in place, setting of targets, and distribution of the initial position paper: it's a case of understanding the audience.

The reporting audience is going to be a wide range of stakeholders.

Communicating the strategy is an important element on maximising the opportunities. That is not just communicating to customers, but to all staff and suppliers. Notwithstanding this, communicating to the wider stakeholder audience too can deliver strong benefits.

Firstly, look at communicating to customers. As discussed, in a rapidly changing market place, sustainability is becoming an important feature to a company's brand and it's strength. By being seen as a responsible and ethical company will draw commitment from the market now and a future market place.

Involving customers into the business sustainability strategy, relationships are being strengthened, creating further differentiation from competitors who are taking very much a Business As Usual approach. Brand development is taking place, to be one that is recognised as a strong, ethical and innovative leader. One that invests, not just in it's products and services, but also into it's staff and customers, it's local community and the community as a whole. A company that cares about the environment, and the quality of life of all those it comes into contact with.

It is highly likely that customers are looking at sustainability, and by collaborating, businesses can develop strategies together, which in turn will lead to new and innovative products and services, which can be used towards the wider audience. Notwithstanding the discovery and exploitation of cost cutting through eco-efficiency focused initiatives.

In a recent report commissioned by DEFRA (Commission on environmental markets and economic performance – 2007) it stated ' *44% of UK based companies state Corporate Environmental Behaviour is influential on improving sales performance.*'

With robust, and provable communication, in terms of position papers at the start of the process, to reporting the first sustainable accounting period, a company is adding value by being proactive and preparing ahead for any regulatory impositions in the future. There is money to be saved, and made, in making changes in a timely and stress free manner, than waiting for the inevitable introduction of mandatory legislation, and carrying out the reports in a rush. The cost reductions add to the bottom line, and communicating the strategy effectively helps support the top line.

Those that do nothing will fall under the Creative Destruction Effect. What this means to businesses, is those who do nothing, against value generated by new players successfully, will be at the incumbent's expense.

So, with customers on board, effective communication of the sustainability strategy will attract new customers who are looking for innovative, sustainable and risk free suppliers. Be proud of what has been achieved, and communicating the continual cycle of improvement through sales and marketing.

The benefits of communicating the work and investment to a new market place cannot be understated. '*33% of consumers investigate a businesses ethical credentials prior to dealing with them*' according to Co-Operative Bank-Ethical Consumerism Report.

Communicating to all staff is vital in the search for emission reduction and cost saving to create a behavioural change. The more aware the staff are, the more they will 'buy in' to the vision, and inspire them to make an environmentally friendly change in their behaviour at home too. This behaviour pattern will have become the norm.

Members of any company are the lifeblood to success. How they are motivated, how they are inspired, and how they engage with each other is how they will engage with the customers. Climate Change is a fantastic opportunity to re-engage staff; as well as customers, through enhanced and innovative levels of customer service.

It has been shown through many studies that staff turnover drops in the companies who take the sustainable route, so saving money. It has also been shown that such companies attract the brightest and the best people; because, the students of today, are growing up in an increasingly resource constrained world; they understand the future difficulties, and most of them will live through them too. That is why they want to work for the right – forward thinking – companies; not any company.

The contribution of the team will always surpass the contribution of the individual. Everyone pulling together will foster a wholly more stable and rewarding culture. This higher emphasis on nurturing and developing team cohesion will improve and go beyond customer expectation and enhance the customer experience – whilst driving important innovation of new products and services further enhancing market share.

All channels are open to a sustainable business. One of the most effective is PR. Local papers (and in some cases nationals) are always on the look out for good news stories. If you have something positive to say, then let them know. Sustainability and climate change mitigation engagement, is a global good news subject: it is not going to go away.

Good PR in the press can save a fortune in advertising and marketing expenditure. And, will further enhance your network. Expand the e-mail database, and what better way of keeping people informed. Free too (apart from the little bit of power to run the computer, which by now, is the most efficient on the market).

For example: a £25m business services and supplies company in the UK delivered some of its sharpest growth during the latest financial crisis and recession (2007-2010). Whilst growing the business by £4m, which they directly attribute to their sustainability credentials, they further reduced their emissions by 50% and saved over £100,000. The free PR the company collected was immeasurable and included:

local and national press coverage and television appearances, boosting their brand, reputation and market exposure.

Delivering the right communication can add great value to any company that demonstrates, lives by, and has sustainability at the core of its business. Sustainability needs to be in the DNA of its operating models, business strategies and critical processes. Through this recent recession, listed companies who are sustainable, on average, have had a share price out perform non-sustainable conscious competitors by around 7% according to the Economist Intelligence Unit 'Doing Good Business and the Sustainability Challenge'. This is not a coincidence; it is a fact of market forces.

Companies who had been asked to rank themselves against peers on CSR and environmental issues in a recent survey and report conducted by The Economist Intelligence Unit 2008 'Doing Good Business and the Sustainability Challenge indicated *'the average net profit growth of the self selected group was 16%, but share growth over the past three years reached 45%.'*... *'At the other end of the scale, those companies that ranked themselves 'worse' or 'much worse' than their peers in social and environmental fields saw annual profit growth of just 7% and share price growth of 12% over the three years.'*

4 OFFSETTING

Offsetting is the method by which the unavoidable emissions can be offset against projects designed and delivered to reduce CO_2 impact. This will be important for company sustainability strategies where the goal is to zero out all emissions: or, just for particular product or service lines. The avoidance is conducted through carbon offsetting, which is investing in projects, typically in developing countries, which are CO_2 efficient, delivering mitigation and sustainability to the communities around them. Therefore, offsetting can develop a sustainability strategy further by not only unavoidable emission mitigation, but also underpinning socio-economic benefits and contributing to bio-diversity protection.

Quality of carbon credits is very important for developing a strong and sustainable governance strategy: the four main features to quality are:

- Additionality: The project only exists because of the investment made from offsetting opportunities, and is beyond business as usual.
- Permanence: delivering offsetting over a sustained period of time, and the project does not erode.
- Leakage: the emissions saved through the project do not get transferred through the initial bad practice being moved elsewhere.
- Avoidance of Double Counting: carbon credits are purchased and retired from the registries: they cannot be sold again.

There are also a wide range of verified quality standards, of which the most popular are Gold Standard and Voluntary Carbon Standard. Additionally, where messages of socio-economic or bio-diversity are important, as they fit within the sustainability strategy and business model, include standards such as Climate Community and Bio-diversity and Plan Vivo: ensuring the delivery of integrity, transparency and quality. It is important, when purchasing credits, the supplier can confirm the integrity through registries. The display of the registry and standard logo's should also be available.

Projects can range from wind farms in Brazil, bio mass power projects in India to small generation hydro in China and, sustainable agroforestry, reforestation and afforestation projects in the Amazon.

However, it must be stressed, that offsetting on it's own is not a route to meet market expectations of a robust sustainability strategy. It has to be first and foremost an exercise in efficiency. Eco-efficiency will deliver the greatest cost benefits in the shortest space of time. Offsetting is the last phase, but no less important.

If the strategy does not allow for wholesale zeroing of emissions, perhaps a particular product or service would be applicable. For example - with every one hundred widgets, a company will plant a tree or invest X amount in a renewable project in India. In this manner the investment is in direct proportion to sales. It follows also, that when applied to an individual product or service carbon lifecycle, with the right balance of offsetting incentive, it would neutralise that stream and demonstrate a direct action delivering value to both supplier and purchaser.

For further details on the range of offset project types, opportunities and standards please see Appendix 2.

5 INVESTOR RISK AND OPPORTUNITY

With constant and increasing regulation and intergovernmental pressure to secure viable and sustainable climate change mitigation, the sense of risk to business is fluid and of concern.

The need to keep to a 2° increase in temperature across the planet means an increase in pressure towards how business is going to conduct itself in the future.

The risk to business is not to do anything. Not to address energy consumption, not to address offsetting unavoidable emissions. Not to engage in socially aware and sustainable patterns of behaviour.

Essentially, to do nothing is a huge risk, and this is how investors view the situation too.

Investors, and that can be banks, institutional investors, venture capital et al. They are all coming under increasing pressure to secure defined limits of risk, and what that risk can place on exposed investment. Fund Managers, with fiduciary commitments to maximise profit for their clients, are also becoming aware of the risk of climate change, and how a company's behaviour is going to expose it to future legislative pressures. Such exposure could therefore reduce the company's shareholder and / or investment value. Through tightening regulations in the future, how much risk is there in a company not doing anything going to impact on the clients future solvency? How much is climate change going to impair a client's asset or income reduction?

Investor pressure towards sustainability is ever increasing. In a 2009 CDP report of investors – 77% of respondents factor Climate Change information into investment decisions citing 'carbon risk' and 'potential regulation' as motivation. These results being very much in line with the Tru Cost report Carbon Risks in UK Equity Funds which stated: "*assessment of future corporate value is directly proportional to carbon and sustainability reporting and management*". Sustainability has become a major protector for companies against: rising costs, damage to brand and reputation, existing and future environmental legal mandates as well as shifting customer and market expectation.

The recent financial crisis has highlighted many areas of weakness. The major being, that global financial institutions clearly did not understand the risks they were taking. Many expert opinions have been voiced on this area, but in short, the sight of the golden eggs was so great, the banks killed the goose to get their hands on the gold quicker. All that happened was the goose died, and the gold stopped.

It follows, risk - has a much-heightened profile. Governments are going to make sure the 2007-2010 situation never happens again. A greater awareness of risk is going to pervade.

The relevance to Climate Change and sustainability: business behaviour is going to be part of future business funding decisions. If a company is in no need of funding, they are exposed to investor pressure through customers and other stakeholders.

A term business will become familiar with, is SRI (Socially Responsible Investment).

At the moment, SRI is typically involved with investment into ethical companies, energy efficient innovation and renewable energy for example. However, we are already seeing a shift from a purely ethical basis - to a basis, which shows a business case for addressing social and environmental issues. Climate Change is seen as a financial risk and there are emerging opportunities in the financial sector involving better governance for developing responsible finance portfolios.

With a greater emphasis on the long view, there is growth in the financial markets towards greater involvement in climate change. Whereas currently, it acts more as a broker to allocate capital for climate change and adoption, thus operating more as a transactional mechanism, SRI is going to drive financial improvements towards the triple bottom line – Economic, Social, Environmental.

But do not think financial institutions are all of a sudden going to become green warriors. However, socially and environmentally astute companies already are mitigating the risks, and grasping the opportunities. Leaving their peers behind.

Fund managers and other financial professionals are concerned with the bottom line; the financial performance of products and services, and they are concerned by anything which may damage such value.

As such, in a recent report issued as a guide for British Pension Fund Trustees, it is suggested that: *"Climate risk can have a real impact on portfolio holdings. There is a growing case for trustees to attain some level of knowledge around these issues, and to take steps to mitigate any negative consequences of not taking action."*

The important message to take from this, is that risk, is seen as a company, not taking any action.

With the growth in national legislation for tackling climate change across the globe, the risks are becoming ever greater. In the UK, the Climate Change Act 2008, Canada – Clean Air and Climate Change Act 2007, New Zealand Climate Change Act 2008, California Global Warming Solutions Act 2006 mandating caps on emissions at 1990 levels by 2020. I will not bore you with a continuing list, but want to draw your attention to the amount of legislation, which is already being passed.

For many company's, there are interests across the globe, and therefore businesses are going to be affected differently from nation to nation. However, consistency across the globe is growing. As we move towards the end of the Kyoto period 2012, this is going to become more real. Governments like to use legislation and tax – polluter pays. It is better to engage now, and make the changes in a quiet and methodical manner.

There is also litigation risk for business through damage that may be caused to the health of people. For the change in a watercourse, and any other form of physical risk, which may be caused to the local environment. With so many companies now having manufacturing and offices across relatively disparate locations, are businesses truly on top of their local environmental issues?

There is also reputation risk. The risk to reputation and brand is a real thing. Business has to ask the question: what if my brand was damaged, what if my reputation was damaged, because I did not address climate issues? These questions any investor is going to ask. And, if there is no demonstration of positive actions being taken, such as: energy and resource management and efficiency, carbon offsetting, asset and brand protection; then investor's are going to score harder on the grounds of future risk.

By taking action, by having a strategy, and delivering a clear message, businesses are demonstrating the quality of management with clear governance. All companies, big and small, face reputational damage, if they disregard climate change and carry on in a Business As Usual manner.

For SMEs, the pressure is rising from both the banking market place - to be seen securing funds for sustainable businesses - as well as customers, who are actively seeking to mitigate risk out of their supply chains by increasingly applying greater demands through greening procurement contracts. This attitude towards informal compliance on sustainability is under-pinned in a recent report from the Carbon Disclosure Project Supply Chain Report 2010 written by A T Kearney, " *members willingness to deselect suppliers for failing to meet carbon management criteria" rose from 6% today to 56% in the future.*

Disturbingly, SMEs are four times more likely to do nothing. This is typically because they see sustainability as a cost, and cite resource constraints. This due in the main, to a lack of understanding of the risk mitigation, value opportunities and business benefits associated with sustainability; therefore, not making it part of future strategy. This being supported by sector associations in the PwC, CDP, DEFRA Review of the Contribution to GHG Emissions Reductions and Associated Costs and Benefits report.

There are a number of new initiatives surrounding the financial sector, which are all relevant to business. One of the largest is the PRI or UNPRI to give it a full title. This is the United Nations Principles for Responsible Investment. It is a voluntary code of conduct, but carries a great deal of weight as it comes within the United Nations remit.

Firstly, it is important to understand that voluntary mechanisms rely on peer pressure, discipline of the market place and sustained NGO demands, to come about. Therefore, do not be fooled into thinking, because it is voluntary, it does not have weight. It does because of the motivation and effort behind the conception.

The principles are a set of guidelines, goals and submissions. The signatories, of which, there are currently, in excess of 500, inclusive of all the banks and financial institutions that are well known, communicate amongst themselves; developing a database of new ideas. They have created drivers towards the information they want to see from companies as part of any potential investment. The collaboration, and the information gathered is then shared. There is an online forum the investment and financial sector share called the Clearing House. Through this, they discuss and collaborate on ideas and practices, sharing information on risks and where they can be found and how they can be qualified.

One of the largest databases of corporate reporting is the Global Reporting Initiative, which the PRI members can access and submit their own reports on sustainability.

Investors, such as institutional investors, have a duty to the long-term best interests of their clients or beneficiaries, known as a fiduciary role. It is now a firmly established belief that environmental, social and corporate governance (ESG) will affect the performance of an investment portfolio.

The level of issues, which may affect performance, would of course vary, being to some extent, dependant on sectors, region, and asset classes. However, it is the recognising of the fact, that, a set of principles would better align investors with broader objectives of society. The investment is very important for the environment, and the communities, but remember to align it to goals and values. Values or principles are consistent with the fiduciary responsibilities of the institutional investors.

Briefly, the principles are:

- We will incorporate ESG issues into investment analysis and decision-making processes
- We will be active owners and incorporate ESG issues into our ownership policies and practices
- We will seek appropriate disclosure on ESG issues by the entities in which we invest
- We will promote acceptance and implementation of the Principles within the investment industry
- We will work together to enhance our effectiveness in implementing the Principles
- We will each report our activities and progress towards implementing the Principles

It is quite staggering the up-take of the Principles since their inception. To an extent, the inclusion of ESG issues, have become a core component for investment decision-making processes for SRI Managers.

The PRI Clearing House plays a key part as to the development of the Principles. And, helped develop the model for corporate reporting.

In order to understand the impact of the Principles further, and get a flavour of the direction; eighty five percent of signatories report that they collaborate with other investors. So, referring back to the fifth principle, this demonstrates a very successful implementation. It further demonstrates the effectiveness of the Principles, their overall implementation, and where business is going to have to be - with regard ESG - when either seeking funding, or being in a supply chain.

Further proof of this direction, through the GRI (Global Reporting Initiative), signatories often report that the lack of information is a barrier to doing business. Additionally, the implementation of the Principles has also lead to over sixty percent of asset owners now including responsible investment and Economic, Social Governance (ESG) in their contracts.

The financial crisis did deliver a great deal of house clearing in the financial industry. And, whilst there were many immediate economic bottom line issues involved with keeping the companies afloat, the majority of signatories have stated that the crisis has actually strengthened their belief in ESG issues as essential information for full risk assessment.

There are many more such investor networks organised as international forums and will be listed at the end of the book for the use of further research and understanding.

The information investors are seeking is in line with a strategic sustainability policy and its reported schedule of actions and achievements. This is particularly pertinent for listed companies, who are more used to including sustainability in their annual report and accounts.

Reporting is a commitment, and a company's statement to stakeholders throughout the value chain. As such, banks are looking at all areas where risk may be involved in the future of the business. For example: what risks are involved with flooding? Is there dependency on stable weather patterns? Commitment to lower GHG (Green House Gas) emissions and the wider issues of environmental impact, investment on mitigation and risk measurement of the supply chain.

For insurance companies, sustainability is going to be essential knowledge for them to be able to underwrite any policy required. From an insurance point of view, they have a double-edged sword, as they will be looking at business from the insurance angle, and from an investment point of view through their own investment portfolios.

If there is a poor level of reporting it would be deemed the business must have climate-related risks. Silence presumes guilt. Because such reporting is becoming commonplace, any due diligence is going to demand reporting as part of the process.

Common sense will ultimately prevail, and reporting will become regulated and obligatory. It is better to get used to it now, and make the preparations for the behavioural change to start saving money whilst creating new opportunities.

Financial reporting laws already require companies to disclose any information that may have a material effect on a company's health, now, or in the foreseeable future. With the adoption of SRI there have had to be an increase in the tools available to make this more inclusive.

For these reasons, disclosure is becoming contractual, and insistent; as climate change is being pursued through inter governmental drivers and the UNFCCC. Hence the emergence of new markets and bodies to create framework around those bodies; hence:

- United Nations Principles for Responsible Investment
- Carbon Disclosure Project
- Global Reporting Initiative
- United Nations Environment Programme Finance Initiative

The reporting wanted is going to follow a framework based around risk mitigation, and a demonstration as to the quality of the management team to understand the risks involved, and what the strategy is to deal with those risks.

As with the Carbon Disclosure Project, investors are looking at:

- Calculation of Green House Gas Emissions

- Energy Efficiency and GHG reduction policy

- Targets

- Mitigation

- Vulnerability to Climate Change

- Emission Trading Activities

- Policies for Climate Change

- CSR

- Achievements

- Strategy

- Land Use Changes

- Pollution Control

- Water vulnerability or source damage limitation

- ISO accreditation for GHG validation and verification

- Integration of climate risks into core business plans

- Energy efficiency investments

- Communication and Reporting

- Ecosystem Services Review

This list of risk areas is not exhaustive but does serve as an indicator of what is to be expected.

For listed companies, such questions on reporting can also come from the point of shareholder resolutions as there is a great deal of evidence, at shareholder meetings, good governance is increasingly seen as the benefits of social and environmental issues being embraced through strategic sustainability policies.

The business and corporate world is absorbing the view that there is a direct link between carbon reduction and management of the wider sustainability issues and return on investment.

Therefore, deliver to the investor market what it wants to understand, such as:

- Strategic approach to mitigating environmental and social risks

- Understanding and taking advantage of the risks

- Illuminate issues which can be translated to bottom line impact risks

- Shed light on long term prospects

- Innovation and market building opportunities

When delivering the report on sustainability also wrap it up in the following manner as an example:

- Give a twelve month + time horizon

- Raw data with sector comparisons

- Discuss the issues in financial terms

- Keep to a business context with past and present performance

- Process for risk identification and management

The reporting guide will demonstrate the management quality in terms of environmental and social leadership and governance. Furthermore, the report will show the level of exposure to emerging sustainability risks, their management and the balance of sustainability opportunities. Because this level of reporting goes beyond what would be wanted or needed in the norm, it delivers comfort, trust and transparency.

However, such reporting is mandatory in some countries such as:

France – Nouvelle Regulation Economique. All listed companies must report on environmental and social information in their annual report.

In the UK, the Association of Chartered and Certified Accountants has published information in the form of the "Guide To Best Practice in Environmental, Social and Sustainability Reporting." It follows; this could act as an excellent reference.

So, it is important to be proactive rather than reactive. To be able to understand, control and reduce energy consumption and other environmental impacts. Mitigate unavoidable emissions. Be more socially responsible. The opportunities are boundless for sustainable growth and profit.

6 CONCLUSIONS

Sustainability is becoming a mainstream methodology to drive cost savings and efficiencies within business. During the worst recession since the 1930s, companies across the globe have struggled to maintain income, and in driving maintenance into company value have initiated cost cutting.

Sustainability has played a part in cost cutting and is not just restricted to those companies, which have global presence, but, as attention falls upon their supply chains, small to medium enterprises (SME) are increasingly under pressure to play their part.

The introduction of sustainability means commitment from the executive board and that commitment to flow through the whole organisation. But where to start has always been the first hurdle to overcome.

It is important when looking at driving sustainability in a company to think of it as a three-dimensional process linked to corporate strategy. This link to corporate strategy gives sustainability visibility, as it becomes part of overall planning, budgeting and accountability processes.

In order to start, it is important to understand where you are, and this involves gaining the data and creating the metrics by which the company is going to be environmentally valued. Then, transform the backward looking metrics into the forward looking tools in order for continuous tracking to create forecasting and delivering action.

Therefore, environmental considerations need to play their part at each level of strategy and governance within an organisation and step across the void between making money and doing the right thing and realising that both points can be attained.

The metrics developed in undertaking the sustainability journey, whilst measuring the environmental and social performance of the organisation, reveal risks and opportunities and so begin the process of improvement. Furthermore, new skills and competencies develop within the organisation in valuing efficiency opportunities from operations to buildings. Hence, sustainability delivers value in cost reduction through eco-efficiency as well as driving new sales and strengthening brand and reputation.

Notwithstanding the direct financial benefits, sustainability also drives innovation as the organisation and its people become used to the balancing act of profit and environment being connected.

So, with an organisation making environmental considerations accountable and treated with the same level of transparency as the financial metrics, it makes the process of tracking true costs and benefits across the organisation and operational activities easier.

This leads to environmental planning and strategic planning working together in understanding what the year ahead and future horizon looks like in terms of accountability life cycle and developing clear key performance indicators and budgets. Additionally, it protects the company from random environmental projects and creates a sustained process with intended actions and clear outcomes and business benefits.

By transcending the duality of environmental concerns and making money, an organisation exposes the false divide between environmental and business thinking.

Whilst business is not typically attuned to the feasibility and necessity of triple bottom line reporting: that of economic, environmental and social, the real truth of the matter lies in using considered environmental metrics and a commitment to work in a three dimensional way. The business can operate successfully and thrive in an increasingly resource constrained world.

Across the globe companies are positioning themselves to become more sustainable and working on the backward looking metrics to understand where they are and get an appreciation of what can be measured, and the value it has to the company as a whole. Yet, many companies, whilst initiating many programmes for energy efficiency, do not integrate them into one coherent policy aligned to corporate strategy, but register them on an activity-by-activity basis.

To create a truly sustainable business is a long-term goal and the creation of a robust sustainability programme is needed to transform business practices to help mitigate climate change.

Sustainability therefore takes and needs commitment from the boardroom to the copy room. The focus and the associated metrics need defining and this means that new information pathways will need opening up. Resources both in terms of time and money will need allocating to create the financial and environmental savings. But the metrics will show the progress.

During the process, the policy will need constantly looking at to see if there is any duplication of effort or any missed issues. And, in keeping with executive buy-in, to encapsulate sustainability, maintain the case by pointing to genuine successes and looking forward at strategic focus areas. This process would underpin the fact that environmental metrics are robust and that the three dimensional processes can be accounted for within the business.

'18% increase in profits for companies demonstrating CSR' (Institute of Business Ethics: - Do Business Ethics Pay? 2003)

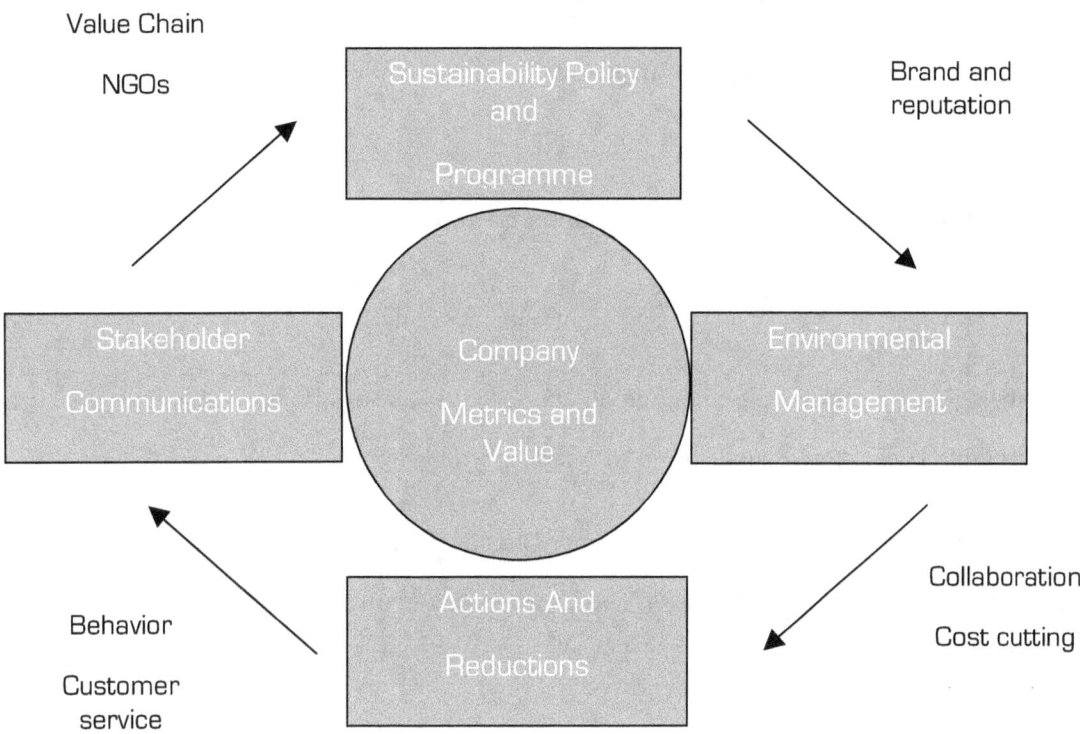

Value Chain

NGOs

Brand and
reputation

Collaboration

Cost cutting

Behavior

Customer
service

The Economist Intelligence Unit – Doing Good Business and the Sustainability Challenge, *'Share price losers are two and a half times more likely to have nobody in charge of sustainability.'*

7 APPENDIX 1 – 8

APPENDIX 1

Infrastructure – where we are going and what it means to you

Many of the new technologies are more expensive than current production yet with scalability and run out, costs can be reduced to keep energy costs in line with current models.

Wind Power for example can deliver energy at zero emission rates and currently there is over 100 GW supplied via wind projects. To give you an idea of scale, the UK currently, from all forms of energy provision, develops 80GW.

Cleaner production of coal-fired power stations can make a significant contribution through technologies such as Carbon Capture and Storage (CCS). It is currently very costly to apply, but again over time this can be made less expensive. Further, coal is still a highly abundant fossil fuel, particularly in the US and China. The fact that it also happens to be one of the dirtiest fuels, the development and deployment of such technology is vital.

Change in land use, with large and small-scale reforestation will also make large contributions to CO2 concentrations when planned and managed efficiently. Notwithstanding the improved environmental impact it adds value and sustainability to developing countries where these projects take place through income generation and wealth distribution.

Other opportunities for land-use beyond agricultural possibilities are the growing of specialist crops for Bio Fuels. New cellulosic bio fuels from crops such as Jatropha, which can be grown in desert areas. Miscanthus, which can be grown in very wet areas. Thus growing such fuel crops in these areas, which are marginal for arable use mitigates the fuel / food debate. With developments in sugar cane, which can be grown well in the southern hemisphere, with technologies such as hydrolysis; ethanol production can be improved by using the leaves and stems, as well as the sugar juice.

Countries such as Ethiopia are already discussing the opportunities these new crop technologies can deliver to the wealth of their country with supply of fuels to the west. This would also deliver increased fuel security by reducing reliance on the traditional supply channels.

So, the targets are set, and we need to aim for a reduction in CO2 emissions to 80% of 1990 levels in order to stabilise the climate. The enormity of the task cannot be under estimated especially as already stated, the growth in population and industrialisation.

According to the Carbon Trust, SMEs in the UK could save a combined £1.37 billion in a single year. There are approximately four million small businesses in the UK.

The EU in 2008 agreed a new target headlining scheme known as the '20:20:20 strategy'. This strategy is designed to increase renewable energy supply by 20%, to reduce emissions by 20% and to improve energy efficiency by 20%.

However, Connie Hedergaard, EU Commissioner responsible for Climate Action, has set a headline target of 30% by 2020 in response to the natural decline in emissions due to lower output through the recession of 2008 – 2010 and as a response that emissions reduction needs to increase to hit the target of 80% by 2050. As stated by Connie Hedegaard European Commissioner for Climate Action Reducing greenhouse gas emissions: a central plank of Europe's climate policy VI International Conference New Energy User Friendly 2010 Warsaw, 18 June 2010

"something needs to be done fast to reduce CO2 emissions and stabilise CO2 concentrations. Business is one of the largest single emitters of greenhouse gases and as such, governments have started placing regulation on business, targeting emissions reduction and mitigation." She went on to say, *" One of the key benefits of moving to 30% would be to restore that incentive for innovation... and*

competitiveness, safeguarding jobs, reducing our energy import bill and boosting energy security, and cutting air pollution and its costs."

Renewable sources of energy supply:

Look at Denmark. As stated by Bill Clinton in his speech at the launch of the Carbon Disclosure Project 2007: Denmark grew its economy by 50% without any increase in energy usage, 'Not one Watt'. Furthermore, it reduced its emissions by shifting evermore of its energy supply to wind.

Whilst at the time of writing, the UK only has 4% of energy supplied by wind power. This resource is set to rise steeply. After all Britain has 40% of the Wind Energy of Europe. Is there a reason why we cannot export renewable energy?

It follows therefore, in Britain, wind energy and wave energy are going to enhance the energy supply of Britain in the future. And switching to such alternative forms of fossil free supply now will only aid the future development through investment.

As wind energy is supplied into the national grid, switching to such a supplier is as easy as switching to or from any supplier. Of course, some of the energy you will be using coming through the grid will be from traditional sources, however, it is the commitment and therefore the message that you can apply to your CSR. Through commitment and communication will come the value.

As time goes on, the distribution of power is going to have to change as the current grid system was designed to deliver power from a central source outward. In the future, it is going to be decentralised and delivered from various supplies and is going to need a greater range of support functions to help manage demand.

A term that will become more widespread in it's use is the Smart Grid.

Smart Grid Technology will allow for the integration of the different sources supplying the grid such as - wind, solar, fossil fuel, nuclear. Smart Software will deliver the power when and where it is needed.

Smart Meters at the consumer's end of the supply grid can then help to optimise your usage of the energy by indicating on an ongoing basis what your usage usage is. The reports generated will be able to tell you what is being used across time, production, and all areas of work. Utilising Smart Meters will be a big move forward in being able to identify waste.

New technology can also be applied locally to your business such as: Solar PV, Wind Power. Where Solar or PV would probably have benefits is in self-sourcing of fossil free power and will be a practical solution in countries where the average sunlight hours is high. In Britain and other such similar climates, the net benefits will have to be looked at in detail.

Innovation is important for all businesses to stay ahead of the competition. The energy efficiency of such new products being brought to market has not necessarily been a prime mover. With how the products are created it is going to become so. For example, a television manufacturer amongst so many, increasingly, the energy consumption of the television is going to become an important factor to the consumer. Like a car (to most people) how much is it going to cost me to run?

The European Commission announced in September 2010 the proposed labelling of televisions and the labelling for refridgerators, dishwashers and washing machines will be updated. As Energy Commissioner Gunther Oettinger said: " *Energy labels move the markets towards highly energy efficient products which is a major contribution to reaching Europe's energy efficiency, competitiveness and climate change goals.* "

This principle is not just for the B2C market. It will also apply in B2B.

Increasingly, as the market consciousness applies it's ethics and how it is perceived as a responsible player, businesses will increasingly only do business with like-minded companies. They will demand more information on the products and services they are buying. Not just in the emission factor in the use of a product, but the emission factor of the product being brought to market.

Labeling will be inclusive of the whole life CO2 emission factor of the product. This will include detailed analysis of- supply, manufacture, use and disposal.

Such labeling creates differentiation. Therefore, will become a driver for innovation. Essentially, for those who continue in a 'Business as Usual' manner will be left behind.

So, what will this mean to you? In short, to do nothing is not an option. In a recent report issued by the Carbon Trust, 'Climate Change A Business Revolution' published 2008, it reported, ' There is a potential 65% decrease in company value if poorly positioned to tackle climate change.'

With the investment you are now making, it is becoming clear where the profit opportunities are emerging:

- Cost Savings
- New Product Innovation
- New Service Innovation

But this is only the beginning. It is important to start communicating your efforts to your customers. They are not only going to be interested in what you are doing and achieving, it is likely, that if they are not already doing what you have advocated, they will be wanting to do so. In this vein, you will be showing leadership. By sharing your experiences with them, you will add value to their business, and further differentiate yourself from the competition. You will demonstrate your true partnership potential.

Communication of your cost cutting and emission reduction efforts, the way it should be communicated has to be credible. It has to be transparent. Therefore, record keeping of sources of the information has to be detailed and what assumptions made if any.

Furthermore, to communicate externally the carbon footprint you need to supply the boundaries of the work, so profiling all data sources and giving transparencies.

In short, as we have discussed in some detail as to the investigation to be carried out, the Carbon Footprint is:

CFP = all materials + energy + waste across all activities of the product lifecycle X emission factors.

It follows:

CFP of a given activity = Activity data (mass / volume / kwh / km) x Emission factor (CO2 per unit)

As discussed earlier in the book, once the GHG emissions are calculated for each activity, they must be converted to CO2e, and this can be done using the relevant global warming potential (GMP). See Appendix. 4.

A service equivalent to a mass balance calculation (as discussed earlier in the chapter) is called an Activity Based Assessment.

For the activity, all processes and materials in and out must be analysed for the GHG emissions.

But, you also want to take advantage of the opportunities replacement equipment will bring you, but money is tight.

Getting loans from the bank might prove expensive, but the costs can be weighed against the savings to be made, and the sales delivery through your project impact. However, there are many ways of being able to fund a shift to a greener and more rewarding business such as interest free loans, which are available through resources such as the Carbon Trust.

There are many other sources of funding, such as applying for awards through schemes such as Shell Springboard. Shell Springboard awards prizes up to £40,000 for innovative new product ideas for enhancing peoples lives through energy reduction. But this should not exclude you even if a new product has not come to fruition. No, because awards can be issued to companies who have driven hard to deliver innovative energy reduction policies.

Other sources of cash are also already at your fingertips such as the ECA Energy Scheme. This is an enhanced capital allowance scheme and is part of the Government's incentive to help mitigate Climate Change. It gives businesses a higher level of tax relief against the investment of equipment which meets published energy saving criteria.

Finally, with regard the assessment of energy flow through your business, it is not just a cumbersome and expensive exercise. If tackled in a positive manner, involving all staff and gaining their commitment, there are huge savings to be made.

APPENDIX 2

Offsetting Projects

It is important to think about what the goals are when offsetting. Offsetting the unavoidable emissions yes, but you must also think about your values. What you want to say to the world about you. About your company, what exposures it may have up or down stream: environmentally, socially or bio-diversity. What you and all the people engaged in the company want to be known for.

Before engaging in offsetting, ask all employees what project areas they see as important. Involve them in the process. Make them stakeholders in the process and not just merely spectators. After all, you have got them on board with efficiency, so don't ask them to get off the bus now.

This whole process is not just about climate change and sustainability. It is also about delivering value and strength into the business too. And, how you communicate it to the world. How you interact with your customers, and the potential customers you are reaching out to.

It follows that business needs to consider a range of options; which, combined, reflect the business and the vision; with values which flow through everyone who works for the company. Therefore, when engaged in business, customers can see a cohesive team, all with a thorough understanding of the business as a whole, and are embedded into the philosophy. It is important for customers to understand this to develop trust.

Rainforests

Tropical rainforests are to be found in areas such as Central and Northern South America, South East Asia and North Eastern Australia. Their importance to climate balance cannot be understated. Furthermore, the abundance of plants, birds, mammals, amphibians that reside in these forests, are critically important to the rich bio-diversity of the planet.

Additionally, they are home to hundreds of indigenous tribes, who have lived and survived amongst these forests for thousands of years. Some tribes, having, still not made direct contact with the outside world.

The destruction of these forests affects the climate and everything and everyone that lives within their boundaries.

Land use change and the destruction of forests is the cause of about twenty percent of GHG emissions. Such destruction has caused a rise of two parts per million CO2 between 1995 and 2005. This compared with a rise of 1.25 ppm between 1960 and 1995 (IPCC 2007b).

Furthermore, rainforests absorb 15% of anthropogenic carbon emissions. It does not take a genius to work out that if we carry on destroying the forests, then climate change will continue un-abated. And the loss of the rich bio-diversity.

At the same time, whilst billions of dollars are invested into new technologies such as Carbon Capture and Storage, our planet has given us the greatest carbon capture and storage technology of all. The Rain Forests. And, this technology is at a very low cost. Because, as with all the points discussed, the cost is, if we do nothing.

It is important to understand the level of destruction in order to understand the importance of mitigating deforestation and degradation. 20000 hectares a day are lost. To give you a mental picture of what this means, it is equal to 1140 football pitches an hour. Forestation already lost is equal to almost the entire landmass of India.

In order to address these issues, there is a growing abundance of projects designed to not only avoid deforestation, but also to look at how this can be maintained in a sustainable and economic way. We must remember many people's livelihoods are also involved in the process. Furthermore, the rainforests are a rich resource belonging to the countries within which they reside. Therefore, like any other resource, such as bauxite for aluminium, or iron ore for steel, this resource must be paid for.

It follows; the projects must deliver not only avoided deforestation but also have positive impacts on bio-diversity and social impacts.

Because the world needs the forests, it does not mean the loss of potential income for the communities whose livelihoods depend on the forests, or the removal of forest for agricultural purposes.

The range of projects available are varied. They involve: tree planting, to absorb CO_2, restoring degraded eco systems and industrial forestry. Furthermore, there are projects for integrating traditional farming methods with local communities; helping to protect and manage existing forests in an ecologically friendly manner. And, within projects, education and the delivery of technical excellence in order that local farming methods may be drastically improved to deliver higher crop yields. Thus, giving greater sustainability on smaller plots of agricultural land taken by deforestation: known as agroforestry.

There are also projects involved with the declaration of protected national parks, designed to deliver climate change mitigation, bio diversity protection whilst delivering an income boost to the local economy and provide long-term jobs. This involves investment through agricultural know-how, and education to the communities as well as paying for the protection of the forests as a natural resource.

The quality of projects is vitally important not just for the project itself in ways such as the assurance of permanence and generating robust monitoring to deliver the community and bio-diversity benefits; but the quality is important to business. Because, with business investment into quality assured projects, the benefits to the company can be delivered in brand, green communication, strength, reputational as well as commercial risk avoidance. And, commitment to the community.

Additionally, quality is important to you for pre-compliance purposes. As and when compliance is applied through, for example, direct taxation on emissions, and therefore, mitigated through emission reduction, the quality of your investment is going to become vital in your offset policy. And, clearly demonstrating the steps you have taken toward climate change mitigation.

Unlike technology-based projects, where direct, verified and accountable carbon credits can be applied, this is not so easy for forestry-based projects. For, some projects, calculated and verified carbon offsets may not be calculated yet, or, estimates given for future offsetting. Particularly when you bear in mind, for reforestation or afforestation, trees take time to grow, and therefore take time to reach CO2 absorption levels. There are of course projects available, where carbon credits have been issued and standards to look for are those such as VCS.

But some projects are as vital through delivery of bio-diversity and community, and the introduction of better agroforestry methodologies, delivering sustainability as well as future CO2 mitigation. An important standard to look for is the CCBS (Climate Community and Bio-diversity Standard).

Many companies are investing in non-carbon offsets such as bio-diversity conservation, community and water conservation. This is because these projects would be more aligned to the CSR objectives rather than the more tangible emission reduction units. It is important for company's to look at and remember what the values are, what is wanted to be achieved with sustainability and what communications will add greatest value.

So, forestry projects can deliver:

- Community and Environmental Benefits
- Deliver mitigation against deforestation and address Climate Change
- Tangibility of offsets with carbon stored in trees
- Protect Bio-diversity

However, location of the project is not important as to its value for climate change mitigation. It is the ability to reduce CO2 that is the important factor. Therefore, project location can be very much determined by personal choice and preference. It may even be decided upon by pure business objectives.

The cost of projects, and the investment to be made in them will vary from project to project. This will be determined by several factors such as – deal size; deal structure, the value of the project and sustainability objectives. For example, currently in the market place, the price for projects, which display a standard, are much higher than a project without. A project displaying VCS for example. Furthermore, some projects are being designed where both VCS and CCBS are applied. VCS, for carbon credits, and CCBS, for community and bio-diversity. These credits, demanding a higher price, because of the value having both standards would accrue to business, and also higher, because of the demanding level of design and investment input to make the project happen.

There are other standards, which at the moment, are little known, such as Plan Vivo. Again, Plan Vivo delivers standards, processes and tools to deliver projects for afforestation and agroforestry, forest conservation, restoration and avoided deforestation. Typically, small holders or communities on their own land, or that of land where they have user rights to implement their projects.

Whilst there is a natural preference for paying for Carbon Credits once they have been actually delivered there is a growing trend towards either – taking out options for future purchase, prepayment for credits or even taking out a stake in the project.

This trend is very important for project development as it helps secure finance in order to make the project happen in the first place and delivers an improved price for the purchaser for making a financial commitment up front.

Giving a small upfront payment gives you the right to purchase credits once they have been issued at a fixed price. This may of course be seen as betting on the rising cost of carbon and the rising cost of forestry credits. The rising cost of such offsets may well be true should such projects become eligible in the future in the US regulatory market place, or even in future phases of the EU ETS. Or even any post 2012 market.

Because of growing trends and market buy-in for companies to be seen to be demonstrating strong sustainability - philanthropic sponsorship of projects demonstrates the investing company to be environmentally progressive. Hence, the market is developing.

Without any payment at the front, there is a financing gap. The project developer may well have to raise funds at the front end, but because CO2 mitigation does not happen for a period of time, the cost borne by the developer may not be sustainable as it may take years to get the investment back. Hence, by purchasing future credits a discount can be applied. However, it is important, that not too heavier a discount be applied as this could well have a negative effect on the project. There is always a balance. The most important factor is the project and what it delivers. The value of the project will deliver value to the purchaser through the story that can be told.

This type of purchasing is more common in the US, than it is to the European Market place. Project developers therefore target the US in a more direct fashion. Furthermore, as has been demonstrated in various survey's, not only are the US more likely to invest with some form of upfront payment, they have so far demonstrated a greater propensity to invest in forestry projects in the first place. Therefore, as the market strengthens, as will credit and carbon prices, so the US will gain the greater benefit.

One area that will be heard and seen more of is REDD. This is Reduced Emissions from Deforestation and forest Degradation.

This has been developed through the United Nations because cutting down forests is contributing 20% of the overall GHG emissions. Furthermore, forest degradation also adds significantly to the overall emissions from ecosystems.

It is set to deliver appropriate revenue streams to make it worthwhile to indigenous peoples to change their forest use behaviour. It therefore promotes sustainable management of forests delivering economic, environmental and socially positive effects on the communities and forest users whilst making a significant contribution to climate change mitigation. It was introduced through the UNFCCC at COP11 (Conference of the Parties) December 2005 towards being included as a post 2012 global climate change framework. Further developed and ratified at COP13 in Bali 2007.

In short, it is set to deliver what we have already discussed for businesses, the importance of the triple bottom line. Whether it is with companies, or the United Nations with whole countries, the focus and effect is the same. The importance of triple bottom line is what is going to deliver the sustainable, profitable future desired. And deliver climate change mitigation.

Be assured, forestry is important, and can deliver significant value to business.

Essentially, cost is also important. The cost of regenerating the world's greatest Carbon Capture and Storage mechanism is a lot cheaper than the technology based solutions we also need to develop.

Some of the greatest thinking on the area of cost has shown, that whilst technology based CCS (Carbon Capture and Storage) could cost as much as €270 tCO2e; reforestation and restoration of soils and degraded land could be as low as €10 tCO2e.

Therefore, reforestation, avoided deforestation and similar project types, show a competitive value on buy-in and can demonstrate maximum effect in terms of value to sustainability. On this basis, they represent excellent value.

So, REDD:

- Set to deliver up to 65% total forestation GHG abatement

- Projects designed to deliver carbon credits for Voluntary Markets

- Robust monitoring for leakage

- Address all deforestation in Asia and Latin America

- Prevent 70% deforestation of Africa by 2025

- Reduce slash and burn

- Reduce conversion to pastureland and cattle ranching through compensation

- Reduce unsustainable timber extraction and compensate

Afforestation

- Set to deliver 13% of total forest abatement of GHG

- Reforest 92 million hectares over next 20 years

Reforestation

- Set to deliver 18% of total forest abatement of GHG

- Replenish degraded lands

- 238 million hectares over the next 20 years

Forest Management (to include Temperate and Boreal Forests)

- Set to deliver 4% of total forest abatement of GHG

- Improve fertilisation

- Fencing to restrict grazing

- Fire suppression

- Improve forest regeneration

In line with tropical forests, lie the areas of tropical peat lands.

Many people are not aware as to the huge environmental benefits of tropical peat lands. These areas are typically waterlogged and so decomposition of vegetation is very slow. Therefore, the peat lands often have an organic carbon content of 30%. Though this is not always the case. Exceptions would be reed beds or papyrus swamps. However, the carbon sequestration and carbon storage capacity is huge. Globally, the figure of stored carbon could be as high as 550 GtC.

This is important to all of us, as marshlands are being drained constantly. And, with the draining and change in land use, large quantities of carbon are released into the atmosphere. These areas are typically drained for palm oil and pulpwood production. Furthermore, the draining allows other organisms to flourish which then in turn expire carbon.

Another common effect with the draining of peat lands, is fire. As we are all aware, peat has been used as a fuel for thousands of years; and, with the draining of peat lands, the peat acts as a fuel; and, sometimes, devastating underground fires can be initiated. Again, releasing vast resources of carbon into the atmosphere.

Losses into the atmosphere as a result of peat land draining can be as high as 0.8 GtC per year. This is a significant percentage of the overall anthropogenic emissions. To give some illustration to this particular problem, there has been some sixty five million hectares of peat land that has been degraded. At 0.8 GtC released, this is equivalent to 20% of GHG emissions for Annex1 countries under the UNFCCC at 2003 levels. In fact, peat fires (especially in Indonesia) are accountable for half the global peat land emissions (Parish et al 2008).

Yet, there are some excellent projects in areas such as Indonesia, which are designed to mitigate such land use change. The projects, in real terms, are typically very cost effective to implement, and therefore can deliver very competitively priced carbon offsets. These carbon offsets which are fully verified and to set standards such as VCS; deliver maximum value to the purchaser.

In contrast; if we continue with business as usual with our rainforests, 87 to 130GtC will be released by 2100. This is equivalent to ten years of burning fossil fuels at our current rates with no abatement what so ever. At the same time, if we are degrading our peat lands, and deforesting to our hearts content, we are also eliminating our resource to absorb CO_2. Therefore, Climate Change instead of slowing will just continue to accelerate.

The sea will try and absorb more, but making it more acidic, so killing off wide ranges of fish species, and destroying the coral, which is home to wide ranges of fish species. There is less fish, so less food, so more hunger, and so more poverty and so on.

Everything on the planet is interdependent, and all has to work well, like any piece of complex machinery. If something goes wrong, the whole goes wrong. Doing nothing is the most expensive decision anyone could possibly make.

No different to a business: as part of modern business terminology is to have joined up thinking. Because, departments are interdependent, all members of the team supply the products and services to customers. So, it is important to stress test every part of the production flow in order to deliver maximum value to clients. Common sense has been around for thousands of years. Joined up comes from a Greek word "Harmozo" meaning to fit together, to join. In it's turn it comes from "Harmonia" meaning joint, agreement, concord. You see, common sense has been around for a long time creating harmony. Harmony to the planet means harmony to your business. It is only a cost if business does not create harmony.

Within the forestry area, other project types to be aware of:

Agroforestry – This delivers the potential for very high levels of carbon sequestration. And, combines delivering high quality and sustainable food production for local communities, combined with modern forestry methodologies. Additionally, these projects are typically strong on bio-diversity and relieve some of the pressure on natural forests so once again improving the capacity for carbon storage.

With well-managed forestry and therefore improved carbon storage, another co-benefit of such projects, is improved and sustainable water usage.

Plantation Forestry – delivers effective carbon sinks, which can sequester significant levels of CO_2. These projects further support groundwater re-charge. But will affect marginal agricultural land and degraded soils.

Boreal Forests – These forests are typically found in the areas of – Canada, Russia, Alaska, and Scandinavia. Because of the typically low temperatures, they have a slow decomposition rate, and therefore are very important carbon sinks, mainly at soil and litter level. In fact, contribute to being the second largest sink of carbon on the planet.

Temperate Forests – are found in – Asia, Europe and North America. These forests are, like tropical forests, home to wide-ranging animal and plant bio-diversity. With high quality of soil, they have suffered under the change of land use for agriculture.

With rapid growth, carbon cycling is very high. And, over the last few decades, many projects have been developed yielding sustainable forests through excellent management practices, which in turn have developed high quality carbon sinks. Such management has lead to the position; that, 7% of Europe's emissions are absorbed by its forests. With constantly improved management techniques, and large-scale reforestation, this position will only be improved upon.

It is important to understand, terrestrial ecosystems store three times more carbon than that of the atmosphere. Tropical and Boreal Forests contributing to being the largest stores, with approximately 2100GtC. Managing these stores is among the highest priorities for climate change mitigation

Forestation projects are wide ranging in project type covering - community, bio-diversity, soil stabilisation, local climate amelioration, recycling of waste products, improved water and nutrient availability, reversal of land degradation, improved livelihoods for local people, eco-tourism, help poverty reduction and, deliver substantial, cost effect climate change mitigation.

Forestry projects deliver to business sustainability contribution: carbon offsetting, enviro and socio-economic independence as well as preparation for compliance, and excellent communication opportunities. Furthermore: mitigation against reputation and commercial risk. These projects are of high value to business because they are of high value to the planet.

In a strong portfolio of project investment, forestry along side technology will deliver great value to business and its value chain.

Think quality, think standards, and think about communication. The most expensive and damaging thing a business can do is nothing.

Biomass

Energy is created from the use of biomass crop residues as fuel. Traditionally, these residues would either be burnt in the fields or left to decompose. But, by supplying these residues to a biomass plant for burning and energy production there are the benefits of greenhouse gas mitigation and improved income for local farmers.

The biomass produces CO_2, however, once burned; there is a measurable and quantifiable CO_2 reduction. The size of the plant will determine the level of CO_2 reductions.

The char that is produced from the biomass burning can then be removed and used as organic fertilizer. This fertilizer can be given back to the farmers who provided the biomass in the first place.

Such plants have many benefits. They offer power supply to local communities whilst maintaining a reduction in greenhouse gas emissions. They provide sustainable jobs to the local communities, and also improve the income base for local farmers. Electricity production replaces the traditional use of fossil fuels. With the organic fertilizer produced, further emissions are reduced by not having to have manufactured fertilizers supplied. Which, would also have to have been transported; meaning: no emissions on fertilizer production; and, no emissions on transport.

Methane Recovery

There are many processes to which waste may be partly made up of carbon dioxide and methane. Furthermore, it is important to remember that methane is twenty one times more potent as a global warming gas than carbon dioxide.

This type of project is typically connected with a factory whose bi-products are methane and other gases that, in traditional terms, have just been released to the atmosphere.

Such projects are designed to capture the methane through its extraction at source or through the wastewater. The methane is then burned to produce electricity or heat or both. The power generated can then be used locally and / or distributed into a main power grid, depending upon location.

Therefore, carbon credits are produced immediately because the green house gasses are no longer released into the atmosphere, but producing power and lowering emissions.

It follows, that other benefits are – improved air quality, improved local income through the supply of sustainable jobs, education through the training provided for local people to work effectively at the plant and further educated in climate change and working towards a low carbon economy. Furthermore, there is independence of power supply, as power is supplied locally to the working communities. There is a huge reduction in the burning of fossil fuels.

Other methane capture projects may involve the burning of gas to produce heat for the factory or the factory processes, so reducing the green house gas emissions. Again, the burning of the captured methane replaces the fossil fuels, which would have been traditionally used.

Heat Recovery

This type of project can be associated with many types of industry. One of the most prevalent is that of cement production. Cement is produced through the burning of calcium carbonate, and is one of the largest, single produces of green house gas emissions.

In the production of cement, a vast amount of heat is produced. And up to thirty five per cent of this heat can be lost to the atmosphere as waste.

So, by utilizing the exhaust gasses, electricity can be generated. The electricity produced helps enable the plant tp become self sufficient in power usage. Therefore, such a project would produce a significant drop in emissions in the form of heavily reduced consumption of electricity from the grid, which, is typically supplied from coal-fired power stations. Particularly, should such a project be based in China, where, over eighty per cent of electricity generation is supplied through coal fired power generation. And, until such technological advances can be made toward carbon capture and storage, this is a very dirty way to supply power.

Hence, in projects such as heat recovery, large amounts of carbon credits can be issued. Additionally to the carbon dioxide mitigation, other very potent gasses can also be mitigated such as nitrous oxides and sulphur oxides. Therefore, delivering significantly improved air quality, GHG emission reductions and contributing to the areas energy independence and boosting the local economy.

Water Treatment

There are many processes where the wastewater emits large amounts of methane into the atmosphere.

However, with the utilisation of modern technologies, such as Up-flow Anaerobic Sludge Blanket Digestion (UASBD), the water to be treated is removed at point of source. The water then flows to another part of the factory complex, where the methane can be captured and burned to produce power. Therefore, very quickly, a large reduction in green house gas emissions can be applied to the project. Not forgetting, that methane is twenty one times more potent than carbon dioxide as a green house gas.

The treated water can then be recycled back for factory use and not released to any local watercourse, improving the local environment. Further, the sludge, formed as a result of the water treatment, and methane capture, can be used as a fertilizer in the surrounding agricultural landscape. And, due to the extraction and burning of the methane, fossil fuel usage is replaced.

Wind Farms

Wind farms produce clean renewable energy. This energy replaces the traditional supply of electricity provided through the burning of fossil fuels, typically, coal. Additionally, wind farms can deliver electricity to areas where there has up to now, been no direct electricity supply, so replacing any future development of fossil fuel power generation.

As there are no carbon dioxide emissions, carbon offset opportunities are once again immediate.

Many wind farm projects also provide the local communities, not just with sustainable power, but sustainable income through job creation, education and other associated environmental benefits.

Look at Denmark. As stated by Bill Clinton in his speech at the launch of the Carbon Disclosure Project 2007: Denmark grew its economy by 50% without any increase in energy usage, *'Not one Watt'*. Furthermore, it reduced its emissions by shifting evermore of its energy supply to wind.

Whilst at the time of writing, the UK only has 4% of energy supplied by wind power. This resource is set to rise steeply. After all, Britain has 40% of the wind energy of Europe. Is there a reason why Britain cannot export renewable energy?

Hydro

By utilising run of water flow in the production of electricity, such projects produce effective carbon reductions on the grounds they do not produce any carbon dioxide in the production of power.

In the absence of such projects, then fossil fuels would have to have been burned in the production of the energy, so adding to climate change.

Again, these projects add to the local economies through jobs and education. But, also through the production of local sources of reliable and sustainable energy, the development of new local businesses and industries is encouraged, developing further, the livelihood to the communities that live within the project boundaries.

Landfill gas recovery

In such projects as Landfill Gas Recovery, the methane displaced by areas of landfill would have traditionally escaped out into the atmosphere.

By tapping into landfill, the methane is drawn off and burned to produce electricity for local surrounding areas, and can be exported to a grid system if applicable.

These projects are important on the grounds of methane potency as a greenhouse gas. The amounts of carbon credits that can be produced are quite significant as they work so effectively toward climate change mitigation.

They also contribute greatly to the local community upon which they are based, through both economical, and environmental benefits. Additionally, they contribute to education through the transference of technology to the local communities so boosting the local skills base.

Geothermal

Emission free electricity is generated through the utilisation of geothermal power which otherwise would have to be generated through the use of fossil fuels; and as such, emitting greenhouse gasses.

A typical geothermal plant pumps geothermal fluid from a reservoir, from deep underground, to the surface from wells bored through the rock. The fluid, which arrives at the surface at temperatures as high as one hundred and seventy degrees or more, is then passed through a heat exchanger. The heat is then exchanged to a secondary fluid, which has a lower boiling temperature.

The geothermal fluid having passed through the heat exchanger is now much cooler. And, at this point, is pumped back down to the underground reservoir via an injection well.

The steam generated in the heat exchanger then drives a turbine to produce electricity.

Because the whole system is closed there are no adverse affects on the environment, and no adverse affects on the geothermal reservoir.

It follows that such projects develop a significant reduction in greenhouse gasses and other pollutants associated with traditional power generation. Further, such power development projects can help stimulate the local economy because of the independence such generation can give.

Some projects use waste heat by supplying it to local greenhouses so developing a local economy for greenhouse agriculture so further boosting the local income generation.

Solar

Found mainly in areas of high sunshine count, solar energy has changed the lives of individuals and whole communities forever. Not withstanding the reduction in emissions and the contribution to climate change.

Such projects replace traditional forms of cooking and heating, eliminating the need for burning of fossil fuels for example.

Efficient and regular supplies of electricity have fostered new entrepreneurial opportunities for the development of new businesses delivering much needed economic growth. With the introduction of new technologies, it has lead to greater education and understanding for the developing world to grow and strengthen whilst following a low carbon economy path.

Solar energy is emission free and delivers the associated benefits. It further has the ability to deliver locally. Where, because of scale, geography and economy, other forms of power supply is just not practicable or desirable. It delivers much needed independence and freedom to communities, which would be otherwise unavailable.

Project conclusions

When considering projects for carbon offsetting and sustainability against CSR it is very important to consider the quality of such credits. Because some credits are cheaper, does not mean they deliver better value for money.

It is important to consider the standards against which the credits are being offered as this is going to be part of the message delivery. Furthermore, it is equally significant to measure them against the values and value chain impact.

When considering any pre compliance, the quality of carbon offsets is vital, as they will be set against international standards such as CDM under the Kyoto Protocol. International standards such as Gold Standard and VCS deliver assurance against benchmarks of – Permanence, Leakage, Additionality and Double Counting.

As mentioned within forestry, some projects may well not deliver carbon credits at the moment but are important for construction of socio-economic and bio-diversity values within the sustainability strategy, therefore, they add value against the triple bottom line of – Economic, Environment and Social. Hence, looking for standards such as CCBS. Additionally, do not lose sight of the fact that forestry projects can deliver carbon credits secured through standards such as VCS. Some projects delivering VCS and CCBS. The number falling into this bracket is constantly rising as joint accreditation is sought.

The list contained within the book are not exhaustive by any means; however, deliver into your hands an understanding of what is available, and the work they do.

They all will add value to businesses and to the position of businesses in the market place.

Full details of any projects should be available from the credit supplier. Being inclusive with stakeholder groups will help to make informed decisions against objectives and avoid making emotional decisions, which may not quite fit.

As Ernest Hemmingway once said *"This world is a fine place and it is worth fighting for."*

APPENDIX 3

Development of new carbon markets

Since the first observations by scientists and the early work dating back to the mid 1950's, there have been the beginnings of concern for what damage industrialisation was possibly causing to the planet, and ultimately this lead to the now famous Kyoto Protocol.

But, the first real step taken to deal with, or at least understand the situation better, was taken in 1988 and the establishment of the Intergovernmental Panel on Climate Change (IPCC).

The IPCC was set up with the primary objectives to understand the science, issues, impacts, and build a consensus on the way forward. Then, in 1992 the IPCC and United nations formed the United Nations Framework Convention on Climate Change (UNFCCC).

This treaty was established and designed to be a formal recognition of Climate Change and a set of non-legally binding targets with the goal to stabilise Green House Gas emissions at 1990 levels.

It was then in 1997 that the UNFCCC adopted the Kyoto Protocol. This protocol is a legally binding set of targets aimed at the developed world countries that ratified the protocol. Not all developed world countries at that time ratified the Protocol, the most notable being the USA.

The aim of the Protocol is to reduce Green House Gas emissions: with targets now set at 80% below 1990 levels by 2050.

Essentially the targets are to be achieved through three mechanisms:

- Clean Development Mechanism.
- Joint Implementation.
- Emissions Trading.

The above Mechanisms allow for Carbon Trading through what are termed Carbon Credits or Carbon Emission Reduction Units. The parties who have signed up to the Kyoto Protocol and its legally binding targets can use these Credits for compliance.

What does this mean?

The Clean Development Mechanism (CDM) is the design and implementation of projects in developing countries. The projects can be in a range of delivering energy where there is a demonstrable net reduction in greenhouse gases. For example, a project could be a wind farm that is to deliver electricity to a town.

The projects are awarded emission credits known as: Certified Emission Reductions (CER's). The, CERs are then purchased, by developed countries, to offset against the emissions they produce. That is to say, the project is delivering energy without emissions, and it is calculated what the emissions savings are. This is done by calculating the energy output against the same output delivered through a set standard of traditional methods, and the corresponding emissions that would have been produced.

Once the emissions savings are calculated, each certified emission reduction unit is given a value, and that is 1 tonne Carbon Dioxide equivalent (1tCO2e). It is these, which are then purchased by developed countries with legally binding targets and achieve offsetting. In other words, if they are emitting 100MtCO2e over their target, then they need to purchase a minimum of 100000 CER's to be on target.

At the same time, the projects have to generate emission reductions that are additional to what would have happened in the absence of the project. It has to be beyond what is known as 'Business as Usual'. This is known as additionality.

The emissions have to be verified and certified by an authorised third party known as the Designated Operational Entity (DOE). The project needs to be verified on a regular basis and the DOE then issues a certificate that the project has not only achieved additionality but also that the CERs are accountable and legitimate.

Joint Implementation (JI) works in exactly the same way. However operates in Annex 1 countries; so, those country's, which have ratified the Kyoto Protocol, and signed up to the legally binding targets. Emissions from JI projects are called Emission Reduction Units (ERUs). The, ERUs can be used by Annex 1 parties towards meeting the legally binding emission targets.

Lastly, we have Emissions Trading. This system is based on a Cap-and-Trade model. Developed countries are issued allowances based on the reduction targets, which have been negotiated. Each allowance given is called Assigned Allowance Unit (AAU) and again equals 1 tonne CO_2.

At the end of each compliance period each country needs to hold an amount of AAU's equal to their emissions over the compliance period.

It follows, that countries, which have reduced their emissions, and are under target, can trade their surplus with those, whose emissions have either gone up, or exceeded their cap.

In this manner, Kyoto has created a new market, which is the trading of CRUs and ERUs as a cost effective way of meeting targets. In turn, this has then encouraged groups of countries to trade amongst themselves. The largest system of such trade is the European Union Trading Scheme (EU ETS).

By being able to trade, countries involved can make decisions on whether they are able to reduce emissions and/or purchase credits to offset. Furthermore, they can also make investment decisions to buy more than they need and sell the surplus at a later date to those who need credits, in the hope that the price for the credits has gone up, so making a profit.

Through this trading mechanism, all the parties involved can look at what is the most cost effective route for them.

Essentially, the EU ETS is the biggest Cap-and-Trade system covering approximately 12000 installations, and by this, about 40% of Europe's and the UK's total emissions. Members can purchase EU allowances (EUAs) or purchase through CDM or JI.

The EU ETS has been in existence since January 2005 and was renewed at the beginning of the second phase (1ˢᵗ January 2008) and so will run until December 31ˢᵗ 2012. A third phase will run beyond that.

There are other trading systems, notably - Norway ETS, Japan Voluntary ETS, New South Wales Abatement Scheme in Australia, Regional Green House Gas Initiative in the US.

They can vary from the EU ETS, for example, with the New South Wales Abatement Scheme; emitters are given a Cap of emissions per capita within the state. If the emitter exceeds their cap they are bound to have to pay a fine (approx $6.25 / tCO2e). However, they can offset the breach of their cap by purchasing New South Wales Abatement Certificates (NGAC's).

The certificates for the NGAC's are generated by projects, which have been designed and certified in the state of New South Wales. Other certificates, which fall under the Kyoto Protocol, cannot be purchased for the purpose of offsetting.

Equally, looking at a scheme in the US, which is the Regional Greenhouse Gas Initiative (RGGI), from January 2009, it covers seven States of the North East and Mid Atlantic and is responsible for approximately two hundred power plants with product abilities above 25MW and using fossil fuels. The power plants can buy offsets, however, they favour the offsets that are generated in the US. Although, other schemes can be used.

Within phase 2 systems, Cap-and-Trade, allowances are either allocated or auctioned off. Each allowance represents a defined emissions amount (SOx, NOx or CO2e). The allowances have been set below what is the expected emissions level creating scarcity so also creating a positive value. Examples of this Cap-and-Trade are: EU ETS, USSOx, and Kyoto Emissions Trading Scheme.

Then there is also the Project Based or Baseline-and-Credit System. This exists where projects reduce emissions beyond a Business As Usual scenario. So therefore, the reductions would not have happened as the project would not be there if it were not for the inward investment.

Baselines are established through obtaining emissions data through various methodologies. Projects reducing emissions through the baseline are entitled to emission reduction credits. These can then be sold to parties who then in turn use them for compliance or voluntary purposes. These credits are typically not issued until the reductions have happened. Examples are CDM and JI.

It is important to understand here how the markets have developed as many banks and traders can purchase emission reduction units in advance. The future emissions have been set out in the design documentation of the project and a price is agreed up front at the start of the project to be paid for at a fixed time in the future for that agreed price.

From these examples, a picture is beginning to clear on how the Carbon Trading markets are working, and work in a very similar way to currency markets and how currency is traded.

In contrast to the compliance market place there is the voluntary market. The players here are different and typically consist of - companies, local government, NGO's, and individuals.

There are various schemes but are not transferable outside the scheme boundaries and therefore are not fungible.

Whilst, the compliance market place is governed by the Kyoto Protocol, there has traditionally not been such an over riding framework in place for the voluntary market place. This not only makes the voluntary market place more complicated and diverse, but also, the credits traded have traditionally not had to pass the additionality criteria either.

However, it is important to note here that there are standards set for the Voluntary Market Place, such as the Gold Standard and Voluntary Carbon Standard. It is these standards, which are important adding value to business and for demonstrating commitment and sustainability.

Having said that, there is a legally binding market for the voluntary sector where the players themselves have set their own agenda and targets. Such is the case of the Chicago Climate Exchange (CCX).

It is a voluntary system and members are set a cap (1999-2002) levels. In order to comply, members have to reduce their carbon emissions or offset generated emissions from projects designed and implemented in the US, Brazil, Canada or Mexico. The projects are primarily focused in areas such as - landfill, agricultural methane destruction, and carbon sequestration in soils or forest-based biomass. This scheme does allow for Kyoto compliance instruments such as CERs and ERUs.

However, to continue with the non-legally binding voluntary market place (the offset market), players are engaged in such voluntary schemes because they want to set their own reduction targets and then offset their own carbon footprint. The reasons for doing this would be to:

- Strengthen sustainability policy
- Address Climate Change
- Engage with customers and employees
- Education
- Corporate Social Responsibility
- Brand Strengthening and Development
- Development of New Products and Services

All these points and others have been discussed.

The voluntary market was primarily aimed at companies and individuals who have relatively small amounts of emissions and therefore set to purchase small amounts of carbon credits from either verified or non-verified projects.

Yet, the voluntary market place over the last two years has seen a steady growth in business. The CCX has seen a growth of 140% year on year. However, growth in this market will depend on the interest from public and all key stakeholders in climate change and also the perception on whether offsetting is the right way to go in the long term.

Furthermore, the voluntary market could be changed at the introduction of regulation and further the introduction of common standards to give further credibility. Or, by evolution of a new climate change policy or agreement by 2012. This does then cause some slight hesitation in the market place while everyone waits and sees. All indicators are that the market will deliver strong growth up to and beyond 2012 as the issues of climate change become more evidenced and delivers greater market understanding.

But, the Voluntary Retail Offset Market Place is still very young and is evolving, and players do need to be very clear as to what their aims and goals are relating to offsets and the wider carbon neutralisation concept before engaging in it.

Yet, in a recent press release from New Carbon Finance, they stated ' *the voluntary carbon markets transacted an estimated one hundred and twenty three million tonnes of carbon credits valued at US$705 million in 2008, up from sixty five million tonnes of credits valued at $331 million in 2007.*' A clear demonstration as to the importance of offsetting and essential investment in to verified projects.

Projects from which carbon credits can be purchased in the Voluntary Sector are typically low emission reductions, and therefore show to be below 15KTCO2e per annum and projects are typically located in developing countries.

Examples of projects in the Voluntary Sector are:

- Renewable Energy   -   Hydro (typically below 15MW)
  - Biomass
  - Wind
  - Solar
  - PV

- Energy Efficiency   -   Low Energy Lighting

                           -   Industrial Energy Efficiency

- Gas Recovery / Destruction -   Methane Recovery from Landfill

                           -   Destruction of HFCs

- Fuel Switch   -   Oil to Gas

                           -   Diesel to Natural Gas

                           -   LPG to Biomass

- Absorption of CO2   -   Reforestation

                           -   Afforestation

A keynote here is that projects, which qualify for the offering of carbon credits, must satisfy the methodologies for additionality. It follows therefore that the projects have shown emission reductions beyond what would have been there under 'Business As Usual'.

The UNFCCC developed a toolkit for additionality and delivers it under the following criteria: 'It is not required under current legislation, it is not current practise and would not be there and economically viable if it were not for the ability of the project to be able to sell carbon credits.'

Every project has to submit details of the predicted reduction of emissions below the baseline emissions that would have occurred without the project.

There are over 60 approved methodologies under the UNFCCC of which some are: fossil fuel switching, gas recovery and distribution, CO2 sequestration, changes in cement production, transport, and reforestation.

Verification has to take place by an accredited, independent third party. It is essential for the verification of the emission reduction to issue carbon credits. The quality of the carbon credits is important as by this measure, value is added to purchasing businesses and demonstrate a clear commitment to projects around the world; possibly mitigating any potential upstream or downstream environmental exposure.

An approved verifier is called a Designated Operational Entity (DOE). They provide written assurance of the verified project emission reductions. This is also why CDM carbon credits are called Certified Emission Reductions.

Another area of importance as to choice of project offsetting emissions is permanence.

Permanence refers to the projects ability in delivering reductions over a substantial period of time. Some projects may not fall under this category. An example here might be Reforestation. What if there was, once again in the future, a change of land use, or the forest burnt down so emitting CO_2 back into the atmosphere?

And so, offset providers should demonstrate some form of guarantee or insurance that if a project were to under perform, then the credits are replaced from other projects in the sellers portfolio or obtain other credits from the market place to cover any such shortfall.

Other drivers may also be where the project developer holds contingency carbon credits back. Also, a portfolio of carbon credits is created from different projects from around the world. This would allow the portfolio to balance any under performing credits that may arise.

Leakage can also play a part in determining the source of carbon credits. Leakage can increase as well as decrease the emissions outside the project boundary. For example, with a reforestation project, what if the agricultural processes, the reforestation replaces, are moved to another area? And now the emissions for that practice are increased because of the move. This increase would need to be set against the decrease of emissions from the project.

The avoidance of double counting is essential too. Double counting can happen where the same credits are sold more than once to different buyers. Therefore, the sellers should have a registry where the credits are accounted for and retired from.

So, credits should always be purchased through a method that uses an official registry, such as Gold Standard or VCS. This route gives surety within the Voluntary Market similar to the compliance of CDM and JI projects as defined by the UNFCCC.

It is important not to lose sight of the fact, carbon offsetting is only one part of an over all strategy to add value to business and the achievement of that value through positive enviro and socio-economic impact reduction combined. Thus committing yourself to a low carbon business and carbon neutralisation.

As has been stated by the Carbon Disclosure Project ' Climate Change is seen as a business risk by 85% of FTSE 500 global companies.' That statement was made in 2006.

APPENDIX 4

Gas name	Pre-industrial concentration (ppmv *)	Concentration in 1998 (ppmv)	Atmospheric lifetime (years)	Main human activity source	GWP **
Water vapour	1 to 3	1 to 3	a few days	-	-
Carbon dioxide (CO_2)	280	365	variable	Fossil fuels, cement production, land use change	1
Methane (CH_4)	0,7	1,75	12	Fossil fuels, rice paddies waste dumps, livestock	21
Nitrous oxide (N_2O)	0,27	0,31	114	Fertilizers, combustion industrial processes	310
HFC 23 (CHF_3)	0	0,000014	250	Electronics, refrigerants	12 000
HFC 134 a (CF_3CH_2F)	0	0,0000075	13,8	Refrigerants	1 300
HFC 152 a (CH_3CHF_2)	0	0,0000005	1,4	Industrial processes	120
Perfluoromethane (CF_4)	0,0004	0,00008	> 50 000	Aluminium production	6 700
Perfluoroethane (C_2F_6)	0	0,000003	10 000	Aluminium production	11 900
Sulphur hexafluoride (SF_6)	0	0,0000042	3 200	Dielectric fluid	22 200

* ppmv = parts per million by volume, ** GWP = Global warming potential (for 100 year time horizon).

APPENDIX 5

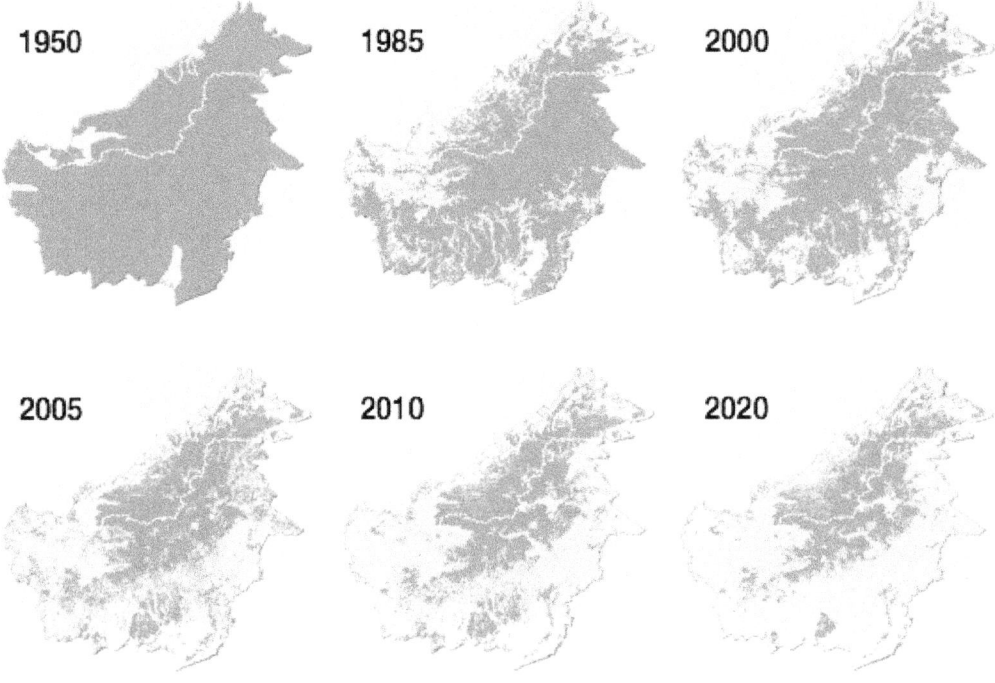

Figure 5: Extent of deforestation in Borneo 1900–2005, and projections towards 2020. Source: WWF.

APPENDIX 6

http://www.savetheorangutan.org.uk/

APPENDIX 7

Websites of further interest

Association of Chartered Certified Accountants - www.uk.accaglobal.com

Climate Community Biodiversity Standard - www.climate-standards.org

Carbon Disclosure Project - www.cdproject.net

Department Energy and Climate Change - www.decc.gov.uk

DEFRA – www.defra.gov.uk

EU Commission Environment - www.ec.europa.eu/environment

US EPA – www.epa.gov

Energy Star – www.energystar.gov

Greenhouse Gas Protocol – www.ghgprotocol.org

Gold Standard - www.cdmgoldstandard.org

GRI - www.globalreporting.org

Interfaith Centre on Corporate Responsibility - www.iccr.org

Institutional Investors Group on Climate Change - www.iigcc.org

Investors Network on Climate Risk - www.incr.com

Plan Vivo - www.planvivo.org

Princes May Day Network - www.maydaynetwork.com

Princes Rainforest Trust - www.rainforestsos.org

THE CMG Consultancy – www.thecmgconsultancy.com

TEEB – www.teebweb.org

UNFCCC - www.unfccc.int/2860.php

UN Global Compact – www.unglobalcompact.org

UNPRI - www.unpri.org

VCS - www.v-c-s.org

WBCSD - www.wbcsd.org

WRI - www.wri.org

WWF - www.wwf.org.uk

APPENDIX 8

Glossary of terms

Assigned amount unit (AAU) A Kyoto Protocol unit equal to 1 metric tonne of CO_2 equivalent. Each Annex I Party issues AAUs up to the level of its assigned amount, established pursuant to Article 3, paragraphs 7 and 8, of the Kyoto Protocol. Assigned amount units may be exchanged through emissions trading.

Abatement Refers to reducing the degree or intensity of greenhouse-gas emissions.

Adaptation Adjustment in natural or human systems in response to actual or expected climatic stimuli or their effects, which moderates harm or exploits beneficial opportunities.

Afforestation Planting of new forests on lands that historically have not contained forests.

Annex I Parties The industrialized countries listed in this annex to the Convention which committed their greenhouse-gas emissions to 1990 levels by the year 2000 as per Article 4.2 (a) and (b). They have also accepted emissions targets for the period 2008-12 as per Article 3 and Annex B of the Kyoto Protocol. They include the 24 original OECD members, the European Union, and 14 countries with economies in transition. (Croatia, Liechtenstein, Monaco, and Slovenia joined Annex 1 at COP-3, and the Czech Republic and Slovakia replaced Czechoslovakia.)

Annex II Parties The countries listed in Annex II to the Convention, which have a special obligation to provide financial resources and facilitate technology transfer to developing countries. Annex II Parties include the 24 original OECD members plus the European Union.

Anthropogenic greenhouse emissions Greenhouse-gas emissions resulting from human activities.

Biomass fuels or biofuels A fuel produced from dry organic matter or combustible oils produced by plants. These fuels are considered renewable as long as the vegetation producing them is maintained or replanted, such as firewood, alcohol fermented from sugar, and combustible oils extracted from soy beans. Their use in place of fossil fuels cuts greenhouse gas emissions because the plants that are the fuel sources capture carbon dioxide from the atmosphere.

Capacity building In the context of climate change, the process of developing the technical skills and institutional capability in developing countries and economies in transition to enable them to address effectively the causes and results of climate change.

Carbon market A popular but misleading term for a trading system through which countries may buy or sell units of greenhouse-gas emissions in an effort to meet their national limits on emissions, either under the Kyoto Protocol or under other agreements, such as that among member states of the European Union. The term comes from the fact that carbon dioxide is the predominant greenhouse gas and other gases are measured in units called "carbon-dioxide equivalents."

Carbon sequestration The process of removing carbon from the atmosphere and depositing it in a reservoir.

CBD Convention on Biological Diversity.

Certified emission reductions (CER) A Kyoto Protocol unit equal to 1 metric tonne of CO_2 equivalent. CERs are issued for emission reductions from CDM project activities. Two special types of CERs called temporary certified emission reduction (tCERs) and long-term certified emission reductions (ICERs) are issued for emission removals from afforestation and reforestation CDM projects.

CFC Chlorofluorocarbon.

CGE Consultative Group of Experts on National Communications from Parties not included in Annex I to the Convention.

Clean Development Mechanism (CDM) A mechanism under the Kyoto Protocol through which developed countries may finance greenhouse-gas emission reduction or removal projects in developing countries, and receive credits for doing so which they may apply towards meeting mandatory limits on their own emissions.

Clearing house A service which facilitates and simplifies transactions among multiple parties.

CO2 Carbon dioxide.

Committee of the Whole Often created by a COP to aid in negotiating text. It consists of the same membership as the COP. When the Committee has finished its work, it turns the text over to the COP, which finalizes and then adopts the text during a plenary session.

Compliance Committee A committee that helps facilitate, promote and enforce on compliance with the provisions of the Kyoto Protocol. It has 20 members with representation spread among various regions, small-island developing states, Annex I and non-Annex I parties, and functions through a plenary, a bureau, a facilitative branch and an enforcement branch.

Common Reporting Format (CRF) Standardized format for reporting estimates of greenhouse-gas emissions and removals and other relevant information by Annex I Parties.

Compliance Fulfilment by countries/businesses/individuals of emission and reporting commitments under the UNFCCC and the Kyoto Protocol.

Conference of the Parties (COP) The supreme body of the Convention. It currently meets once a year to review the Convention's progress. The word "conference" is not used here in the sense of "meeting" but rather of "association," which explains the seemingly redundant expression "fourth session of the Conference of the Parties."

Deforestation Conversion of forest to non-forest.

Emission reduction unit (ERU) A Kyoto Protocol unit equal to 1 metric tonne of CO_2 equivalent. ERUs are generated for emission reductions or emission removals from joint implementation project.

Emissions trading One of the three Kyoto mechanisms, by which an Annex I Party may transfer Kyoto Protocol units to or acquire units from another Annex I Party. An Annex I Party must meet specific eligibility requirements to participate in emissions trading.

European Union (EU) As a regional economic integration organization, the EU is a Party to both the Convention and the Kyoto Protocol. However, it does not have a separate vote from its member states. Because the EU signed the Convention when it was known as the EEC (European Economic Community), the EU retains this name for all formal Convention-related purposes. Members are Austria, Belgium, Cyprus, Czech Republic, Denmark, Estonia, Finland, France, Germany, Greece, Hungary, Ireland, Italy, Latvia, Lithuania, Luxembourg, Malta, the Netherlands, Poland, Portugal, Slovakia, Slovenia, Spain, Sweden, and the United Kingdom.

Fugitive fuel emissions Greenhouse-gas emissions as by-products or waste or loss in the process of fuel production, storage, or transport, such as methane given off during oil and gas drilling and refining, or leakage of natural gas from pipelines.

Global warming potential (GWP) An index representing the combined effect of the differing times greenhouse gases remain in the atmosphere and their relative effectiveness in absorbing outgoing infrared radiation.

Greenhouse gases (GHGs) The atmospheric gases responsible for causing global warming and climate change. The major GHGs are carbon dioxide (CO_2), methane (CH_4) and nitrous oxide (N_2O). Less prevalent –but very powerful – greenhouse gases are hydrofluorocarbons (HFCs), perfluorocarbons (PFCs) and sulphur hexafluoride (SF_6).

HFC Hydrofluorocarbons.

ICCP International Climate Change Partnership.

ICLEI International Council of Local Environmental Initiatives.

IEA International Energy Agency.

IGO Intergovernmental organization.

IMO International Maritime Organization.

Intergovernmental Panel on Climate Change (IPCC) Established in 1988 by the World Meteorological Organization and the UN Environment Programme, the IPCC surveys world-wide scientific and technical literature and publishes assessment reports that are widely recognized as the most credible existing sources of information on climate change. The IPCC also works on methodologies and responds to specific requests from the Convention's subsidiary bodies. The IPCC is independent of the Convention.

International Climate Change Partnership Global coalition of companies and trade associations committed to constructive participation in international policy making on climate change.

IOC Intergovernmental Oceanographic Commission.

ISO International Standards Organization.

Joint implementation (JI) A mechanism under the Kyoto Protocol through which a developed country can receive "emissions reduction units" when it helps to finance projects that reduce net greenhouse-gas emissions in another developed country (in practice, the recipient state is likely to be a country with an "economy in transition"). An Annex I Party must meet specific eligibility requirements to participate in joint implementation.

Kyoto Protocol An international agreement standing on its own, and requiring separate ratification by governments, but linked to the UNFCCC. The Kyoto Protocol, among other things, sets binding targets for the reduction of greenhouse-gas emissions by industrialized countries.

Kyoto mechanisms Three procedures established under the Kyoto Protocol to increase the flexibility and reduce the costs of making greenhouse-gas emissions cuts; they are the Clean Development Mechanism, Emissions Trading and Joint Implementation.

Land use, land-use change, and forestry (LULUCF) A greenhouse gas inventory sector that covers emissions and removals of greenhouse gases resulting from direct human-induced land use, land-use change and forestry activities.

Leakage That portion of cuts in greenhouse-gas emissions by developed countries – countries trying to meet mandatory limits under the Kyoto Protocol – that may reappear in other countries not bound by such limits. For example, multinational corporations may shift factories from developed countries to developing countries to escape restrictions on emissions.

Mitigation In the context of climate change, a human intervention to reduce the sources or enhance the sinks of greenhouse gases. Examples include using fossil fuels more efficiently for industrial processes or electricity generation, switching to solar energy or wind power, improving the insulation of buildings, and expanding forests and other "sinks" to remove greater amounts of carbon dioxide from the atmosphere.

Montreal Protocol The Montreal Protocol on Substances that Deplete the Ozone Layer, and international agreement adopted in Montreal in 1987.

N2O Nitrous oxide.

Non-Annex I Parties Refers to countries that have ratified or acceded to the United Nations Framework Convention on Climate Change that are not included in Annex I of the Convention.

Non-governmental organizations (NGOs) Organizations that are not part of a governmental structure. They include environmental groups, research institutions, business groups, and associations of urban and local governments. Many NGOs attend climate talks as observers. To be accredited to attend meetings under the Convention, NGOs must be non-profit.

Non-paper An in-session document issued informally to facilitate negotiations. A non-paper does not have an official document symbol. It may have an identifying number or carry the name of its author.

OECD Organisation for Economic Co-operation and Development.

OPEC Organization of Petroleum Exporting Countries.

Party A state (or regional economic integration organization such as the European Union) that agrees to be bound by a treaty and for which the treaty has entered into force.

PFC Perfluorocarbon.

Protocol An international agreement linked to an existing convention, but as a separate and additional agreement which must be signed and ratified by the Parties to the convention concerned. Protocols typically strengthen a convention by adding new, more detailed commitments.

Reforestation Replanting of forests on lands that have previously contained forests but that have been converted to some other use.

Reservoirs A component or components of the climate system where a greenhouse gas or a precursor of a greenhouse gas is stored. Trees are "reservoirs" for carbon dioxide.

Removal unit (RMU) A Kyoto Protocol unit equal to 1 metric tonne of carbon dioxide equivalent. RMUs are generated in Annex I Parties by LULUCF activities that absorb carbon dioxide.

SF6 Sulphur hexafluoride.

Second Assessment Report (SAR) An extensive review of worldwide research on climate change compiled by the IPCC and published in 1995. Some 2,000 scientists and experts participated. The report is also known as Climate Change 1995. The SAR concluded that "the balance of evidence suggests that there is a discernible human influence on global climate." It also said "no-regrets options" and other cost-effective strategies exist for combating climate change.

Sink Any process, activity or mechanism which removes a greenhouse gas, an aerosol or a precursor of a greenhouse gas from the atmosphere. Forests and other vegetation are considered sinks because they remove carbon dioxide through photosynthesis.

Special Climate Change Fund (SCCF) The SCCF was established to finance projects relating to adaptation; technology transfer and capacity building; energy, transport, industry, agriculture, forestry and waste management; and economic diversification. This fund should complement other funding mechanisms for the implementation of the Convention. The Global Environment Facility (GEF), as the entity that operates the financial mechanism of the Convention, has been entrusted to operate this fund. For more information

"Spill-over effects" Reverberations in developing countries caused by actions taken by developed countries to cut greenhouse-gas emissions. For example, emissions reductions in

143

developed countries could lower demand for oil and thus international oil prices, leading to more use of oil and greater emissions in developing nations, partially off-setting the original cuts. Current estimates are that full-scale implementation of the Kyoto Protocol may cause 5 to 20 per cent of emissions reductions in industrialized countries to "leak" into developing countries.

Sustainable development Development that meets the needs of the present without compromising the ability of future generations to meet their own needs.

Third Assessment Report (TAR) The third extensive review of global scientific research on climate change, published by the IPCC in 2001. Among other things, the report stated that "The Earth's climate system has demonstrably changed on both global and regional scales since the pre-industrial era, with some of these changes attributable to human activities. There is new and stronger evidence that most of the warming observed over the last 50 years is attributable to human activities." The TAR also focused on the regional effects of climate change.

Track- two JI One of two approaches for verifying emission reductions or removals under joint implementation, whereby each JI project is subject to verification procedures established under the supervision of the Joint Implementation Supervisory Committee. Track two procedures require that each project by reviewed by an accredited independent entity.

UN United Nations.

UNCCD United Nations Convention to Combat Desertification.

UNCED United Nations Conference on Environment and Development.

UNCTAD United Nations Conference on Trade and Development.

UNDP United Nations Development Programme.

UNECE United Nations Economic Commission for Europe.

UNEP United Nations Environment Programme.

UNFCCC United Nations Framework Convention on Climate Change.

UNIDO United Nations Industrial Development Organization.

Uniform report format A standard format through which Parties submit information on activities implemented jointly under the Convention.

Voluntary commitments A draft article considered during the negotiation of the Kyoto Protocol that would have permitted developing countries to voluntarily adhere to legally binding emissions targets. The proposed language was dropped in the final phase of the negotiations. The issue remains important for some delegations and may be discussed at upcoming sessions of the Conference of the Parties.

Vulnerability The degree to which a system is susceptible to, or unable to cope with, adverse effects of climate change, including climate variability and extremes. Vulnerability is a function of the character, magnitude, and rate of climate variation to which a system is exposed, its sensitivity, and its adaptive capacity.

WCC World Climate Conference.

WEOG Western European and Others Group (United Nations regional group).

WHO World Health Organization.

WMO World Meteorological Organization.

WSSD World Summit on Sustainable Development.

WTO World Trade Organization.

Glossary of Terms: UNFCCC

ABOUT THE AUTHOR

Christopher is principle of The CMG Consultancy and has been in business development for over 25 years; having developed a range of businesses across various sectors, from developing training courses bridging the gap between corporate strategy and IT development whilst additionally leading the way in energy and cost reduction fleet management solutions as far back as the mid 90s. He is a leading advocate of sustainability having written training courses bridging the gap between corporate strategy and sustainability, and is a regular public speaker on the subject. Additionally, Christopher has been an active member of the stakeholder advisory group for the Greenhouse Gas Protocol product and supply chain initiative as well as many other global groups, such as GRI Global Reporting and the Prince's Mayday Network.

The CMG Consultancy is playing a leading role in the development and deployment of sustainability strategy and planning, and designing communications solutions across the range of stakeholder groups e.g. suppliers, investors, customers, top down employee groups. By emhedding sustainability into the DNA of organisations, this initiates change through a continual cycle of improvement; developing long term results by reducing environmental and cost impact on organisational value, by setting wide ranging KPIs from establishing the current status of sustainability and, through creating the metrics, by which the organisation is going to be environmentally and socially valued.

CMG THE CMG Consultancy ■   Plot - Plan - Perform

www.thecmgconsultancy.com

www.ingramcontent.com/pod-product-compliance
Lightning Source LLC
Chambersburg PA
CBHW081352280526
45788CB00009B/2854